WOMAN'S OWN
Pot Plant Doctor

Hazel Evans and Alan Kumm

Hamlyn

London · New York · Sydney · Toronto

First published in 1978 by
The Hamlyn Publishing Group Limited
Astronaut House, Feltham, Middlesex, England
Second impression 1978

Filmset in England by Filmtype Services Limited, Scarborough
in 11 on 13pt Monophoto Times
Printed in England by Hazell Watson & Viney Limited,
Aylesbury, Bucks

ISBN 0 600 37150 6

Line drawings by Barry Wilkinson

Contents

Introduction

When Woman's Own magazine asked us, some time ago, to do a phone-in on house-plant problems, we didn't realise just what we were in for as we walked unsuspectingly into the office in Covent Garden that was to be our virtual home for a week.

Four days later, almost speechless, exhausted beyond belief, we tottered out – even Alan, who is an ex-disc jockey, had run out of words. For the switchboard was jammed from first thing in the morning until the office closed. Lights winked relentlessly at us from it as we put down the phone on one call and took up another. We had half-hour chats with Dublin, long calls from Manchester, ladies in Land's End who had trouble with their begonias – what your telephone bills must have been like afterwards, we simply dread to think!

We made some good friends – some of you phoned us more than once for a chat – and we disappointed a lot of people who were simply unable to get through. And we came across some problems that, quite frankly, stumped us at the time, though we've made a point of finding out the answers since. Certain things came up again and again: 'My Swiss Cheese Plant hasn't got any holes in it.' . . . 'My Rubber Plant is dropping its lower leaves.' . . . 'My Spider Plant hasn't got any babies.' And out of it all came the idea for this book, because your telephone calls showed, only too plainly, that while there are a lot of books on sale about house plants, there doesn't seem to be anything specifically on house-plant problems. There was a real need for something to help you trace what was wrong, and tell you how to put it right.

We've tried to make it entertaining reading as well, for we soon came to realise from talking to you, that for you, as for us, house plants are something more than just plants – they're pets.

They're alive, and they're just as responsive to attention and affection as any animal. And if you give them sufficient care, and take a little trouble, they will flourish and brighten your home as nothing else can do.

All plants need time spent on them, but some need much more than others. What came over loud and clear in our conversations with you, the house-plant enthusiasts, was that all too often you hadn't chosen the right plant in the first place. It's only too easy to be impressed by an exotic but temperamental plant in someone else's home or in a shop and say 'that's for me', but is it? Lesson number one: before you walk away with a plant from the florist's shop or the garden centre read the label (more and more plants now have informative labels on them) or, if there isn't one, ask questions. Like everything else, house plants have rocketed in price and to have one die on you is an expensive mistake.

It pays, too, to shop around a little, especially if you're planning to buy several plants. Take a general view of the place where they are on sale: is the general effect that of a rather tatty set of plants, probably bought in from somewhere else and simply put out for sale? There are some very good, reputable 'brand name' plants around which come from specialist growers, and which will be in tip-top condition, but there are, at the same time, house plants that haven't had such a careful upbringing and have been raised under less suitable conditions and shipped out for sale.

Start off with a sound-looking plant. Don't be fobbed off by anything that appears stunted or sickly. Remember that height is not everything, a good plant will have a well-balanced selection of leaves on it, not all huddled together at the top or bottom. However tall they may be avoid plants with spindly stalks and leaves set wide apart – a short, stocky, bushy plant is much better.

Pass up a plant that has both very large and very small leaves on it. It has probably been force-fed to get it on sale fast. The leaves will tell you more about the plant than anything else: steer clear of curling or drooping leaves, check out the undersides for pests. Don't touch anything that has yellowing lower leaves as that is probably a sign of bad care in the nursery. Don't buy plants with leaves that are going brown round the edges, however cheap they are, there could be any number of causes for that. The leaves should look crisp and shiny; if they are dusty then the plant may have been neglected.

Check that the plant looks right in its pot. If it appears top-heavy, it may be pot-bound; turn the plant upside down carefully and see if there are any roots poking out through the drainage holes of the container. In some places we've seen plants on sale that have actually got roots growing through the pot and into the tray underneath, a clear sign that the plant is badly pot-bound and, therefore, neglected. Check the soil round the base of the plant too, if it is caked then you may have root problems.

When you make your purchase, don't, if you're a first-timer, buy too many different plants at once or you'll be driven mad trying to cope with their different requirements. Plants are like people, there's no doubt about that, and tests done on them with a lie detector have shown that plants actually 'sweat' with fear when they are threatened. There's still a lot we don't know about the plant world and plant behaviour, and lots more to find out.

How to Use This Book

It is divided into six sections. The first one deals with the most common disorders that you're likely to come across, the second purely with pests – and there are quite a few that can clobber your poor plants, especially in hot, dry conditions. The third section deals with plants that need special treatment of some kind or other, they're not necessarily difficult to grow – just different.

Then we have a section on planting and general care which also offers advice on planting a hanging basket and a bottle garden. This is followed by a special section on propagation – how to have more plants for free. Finally, we round up the book with some ideas on special plants for special places – and people. Happy reading!

Be Your Own Plant Doctor
...with our Instant Diagnosis Chart

Problem	Cause	Remedy
General Appearance		
Plant droops and won't grow. Dull foliage and yellowing leaves.	Not enough water.	First aid: immerse pot in tepid water for one minute. Afterwards water more often *or* increase amount of water.
Plant droops. Soft stem, wilted leaves or dropping leaves.	Too much water.	Allow plant to dry out. Pick off yellow leaves. Put in shady spot outdoors to recuperate in summer.
New plant unhappy-looking.	Change of environment.	Allow to settle by finding out its basic need for light, watering, temperature and humidity.
Plant lacks vigour and doesn't grow. Colour fades with yellowing leaves turning brown at tips. Older leaves drop.	Underfeeding. May need repotting. Air pollution and draughts. Natural ageing process.	Start feeding with half-strength fertiliser. Repot if necessary. For brown tips feed with Sequestrene–iron chelate. Move to new position.
Plant dying off, while new growth is blackened and misshapen.	Overfeeding.	Immerse pot in tepid water for one minute.
Slow growth.	Overwatering. Too low light. Wrong temperatures/humidity. Crowded pot/wrong soil. Dormant period.	Dry out pot. Move nearer bright window. Adjust. Repot. Place in cooler room.
Plant wilts frequently, fades or burns.	Too much light.	Move away from window-sill.
Plant gets leggy and droops. Leaves yellow and fall off.	Too low light.	Move towards better light in easy stages.
Plant not growing well and has no lustre. Dry and crackling leaves.	Not enough humidity. Red spider mite.	Group similar plants together. Mist spray with water. Use systemic insecticide.
Plant wilts.	Wrong watering. Poor drainage or compacted soil. Wrong temperature or low humidity.	Plunge into tepid water for one minute. Repot and improve drainage with crocks at bottom of pot. Adjust; put with other similar plants to recuperate.
Collapsed plant.	Overwatering. Draughts.	Allow to dry out: stir soil surface with a fork. Change situation.
Root deterioration, indicated by plant wilting.	Overwatering; root rot disease. Overfeeding. Poor drainage.	Allow plant to dry out. Don't feed for several weeks. Repot.

Problem	Cause	Remedy
continued from page 6	Earthworms, if garden soil used for potting soil.	Repot using sterilised proprietary composts.
Broken stem or branches.	Pet or accidental damage.	Use splint and sticky tape as first aid. Otherwise take cuttings for propagation.
Leaf Indicators		
Curled and dropped leaves.	Overwatering.	Allow to dry out and hasten the operation by stirring compost surface with a fork to aerate.
	Low temperatures.	Check plant's requirements and place in correct situation to speed recovery.
	Draughts.	Move to draught-free situation.
Older leaves drop.	Underwatering.	Gradually step up amount. If possible use rainwater at tepid temperature.
	Low light.	Move in stages nearer window or help with artificial light.
	Underfeeding.	Increase fertiliser, but at only half the manufacturer's suggested dosage.
	Compacted soil.	Repot.
	Too high temperature. Natural ageing process.	Check plant's needs and move.
Most leaves drop.	Underwatering.	Gradually increase supply but be ready to stop temporarily if signs appear of overwatering.
	Low light.	Move table lamp close by and give several hours extra light each day to start with. Extend time if necessary.
	Overfeeding.	Cut back on giving regular doses of fertiliser for several weeks.
	Temperature swing.	Change position.
Spongy, sodden new leaves.	Overwatering.	Allow plant to dry out. Repotting in a similar size pot with a little drier compost is sometimes employed as an emergency technique.
Soft rotten leaf tissue.	Overwatering. Too high humidity.	Allow plant to dry out. Open a few doors and windows if possible to get air movement, or get a fan operating.
Dry, depressed leaf spots.	Anthracnose disease.	Fungicide spray.
Moist, blistered leaf.	Leaf spot disease.	Move plant to less humid position that is light and dry. Spray with fungicide.
Burnt spots.	Water droplets on leaf act as a magnifying glass to sun's rays.	Be more careful with routine watering; check watering can spout is *under* leaves.
Crisp, brown leaf spots.	Overwatering. Overfeeding. Air pollution.	Allow plant to dry out. Curtail feeding for several weeks. Move plant away from coal fires, paraffin fumes, etc.
Small yellow leaf spots.	Mites, scale.	Wipe off with soapy water. Spray with malathion.
	Incorrect feeding.	Check plant's need.
	Leaf spot disease.	Spray with fungicide.
Leaf tips brown and die off.	Anthracnose disease. Overwatering. Too little light.	Foliar fungicide spray. Plant must be allowed to dry out. Move nearer window or supplement with artificial light.

Problem	Cause	Remedy
Continued from page 7	Too warm temperatures.	Move away from south- or west-facing window to an east-facing window where temperatures shouldn't rise so much.
	Sun scorch.	Screen with net curtain.
	Air pollution.	Move away from room if there's a gas or coal fire.
	Overfeeding.	Reduce regular feeding for several weeks.
Pale leaves.	Mites.	Soap-and-water wash. If the plant is too infected get rid of it.
	Lack of light.	Check plants needs and adjust.
	Underfeeding.	Give a feed, but start at about half-strength.
	Underwatering.	Gradually increase amount of water; don't be too enthusiastic.
Yellow along leaf veins.	Incorrect feeding.	Check if your feeding programme is too spartan.
	Soil too alkaline.	Sequestrene (iron chelate) will remedy this problem.
Soft, blackish patches on leaves.	Overwatering.	Curb your kindness: you will kill this plant. Allow to dry out.
White felt-like coating on leaves.	Mildew, most likely from overwatering.	Make sure there's adequate circulation of air; burn affected leaves. Spray with captan or benomyl.
Grey cast to leaves.	Too much light.	Not a major problem; always check on plant's specific needs – it might require adequate but shaded light.
Sticky substance on leaves.	Aphids.	Sponge with tepid water with a little detergent, then rinse with clean water. Dose with malathion and spray with water occasionally. Use systemic insecticide.
Holes in leaves.	Slugs, caterpillars, accidental damage.	Pick off any foreigners on the plant.
Sooty black patches.	Fungus attached to sticky parts of plant's stem caused by aphid feeding action.	Spray with malathion.
Winding trails on leaves.	Leaf miners – the larvae of a variety of flies that eat leaf tissue.	Remove infected leaves. Use systemic insecticide. Always obey manufacturer's instructions and don't overdose.
Papery scars on leaves.	Thrips.	Remove infected leaves. Spray with malathion or derris.
Leaves rolled inwards at tips.	Leaf rollers.	Affects indoor roses and begonias. Pick off infested leaves. Spray with malathion.
Variegated leaves lose colour.	Too low temperature.	Adjust.
	Low light.	Give extra 'daylight' from table lamp or strip light.

Flowers

Buds drop.	Change in environment.	Don't move pot or turn it.
	Low humidity.	Place on saucer of pebbles with water or moist peat bed.

Problem	Cause	Remedy
Continued from page 8	Underwatering.	Carefully increase amount of water.
	Mites, thrips, whitefly.	Spray with malathion.
	Air pollution.	Remove from room if gas or coal fires in use.
Flowers do not last.	Underwatering.	Gradually increase amount of water.
	Too high temperatures.	Move to cooler environment.
	Bad light.	Place nearer window or use artificial light.
	Plant may have specific needs.	Check plant's pedigree.
Poor colour.	Too low light.	Move to brighter window; often an easterly window is ideal.
No flowers (on a flowering plant!)	Too low light.	Move to a window.
	Wrong day-length.	Adjust daylight shortage by use of lamp or strip light.
	Thrips.	Spray with malathion.
	Bulb pests.	Examine closely before planting.
Deformed flowers.	Thrips.	Spray with malathion.
Flowers brown and shrivelled.	Underwatering.	Carefully increase supply, checking adequate drainage.
Indoor daffodil/tulip flowers don't appear on time.	Not specially prepared in cold store for early flowering.	Buy properly prepared bulbs from dealer. Garden collected bulbs aren't suitable.
Crown rotted or stem rotted.	Overwatering.	Drastically reduce water supply. Pinch out flowers. Repot.
	Excess humidity.	Allow air to circulate.
	Wrong temperatures.	Adjust to plant's needs.
Mildews.	Damp or over humidity.	Allow air to circulate.
	Overcrowding of plants.	Separate plants.
	Overwatering.	Reduce amount of watering, cut away badly affected leaves.
Seedlings collapse.	Damping-off disease.	Discard and start again with sterilised soil.

Insects

Problem	Cause	Remedy
New growth eaten.	Slugs and caterpillars, ants.	Pick off offenders.
Brown hard discs.	Scale.	Early observation will save plant. Wipe off with soapy water. Spray with malathion.
White fuzz on leaves and stem.	Mealy bugs.	Remove with alcohol or methylated spirits on a swab. Apply systemic sprays.
Spider webs, leaf speckling.	Red spider mites.	Spray with cold water to remove pests. Use systemic insecticide.
Excrement specks.	Caterpillars, thrips.	Mild infestations can be controlled by spraying with tepid soapy water. Then spray with malathion. Pick off caterpillars.
Shining trails on leaves and pots.	Slugs.	You won't get many indoors; pick off.
Seed-like particles under leaves or 'cigarette-ash' appearance.	White fly.	Soapy water wash for mild attacks. Spray with malathion or general insecticide on plant after placing it inside large plastic bag.

Common Disorders

A happy, healthy plant, growing in the right environment and well looked after, should be able to shrug off most attacks by pests and viruses. In fact most of the problems that arise with house plants are the direct result of people not knowing just how to care for them. So before you buy a house plant, do your homework: find out its basic needs. You may fancy a specific plant to jazz up the look of a room, but if that room can't give it the right amount of heat, light, and humidity, then it is doomed before you bring it home.

Overwatering – The Killer Disease

Most of us kill our house plants with kindness rather than neglect. There's no doubt at all that the most common disorder on the house plant front is overwatering. In fact it has been estimated that this is the reason for at least 75 per cent of all indoor plant deaths. The only likely exception to the rule is the unlucky fate of the 'shared' plant, one that is grown in an office or factory and is nobody's property and yet everybody's property at the same time, and can quite easily wilt and then die off from sheer neglect before everyone's eyes. Underwatering is much easier to spot – you usually realise that you've neglected the plant a bit – and it's much easier to put right if things haven't gone too far: a good drink is all that is required. Overwatering needs more drastic first aid (see page 21) as in a bad case the plant can actually collapse. Tell-tale signs include puddles of water staying on the surface of the compost some time after you've given the plant a drink, moss-like growth on the top of the soil, and, very often, yellowing leaves.

Get the Light Right

Some plants can stand a lot less light than others, but *no* plant can grow in near darkness. They need sunlight or good artificial light to manufacture food in their leaves. But, on the other hand, that doesn't mean that they are necessarily happy sitting on a window-sill. Most plants prefer a general brightness rather than direct sun. They will soon show you if they're not getting enough by becoming straggly and pallid.

Humidity Helps – a Lot

Lots of diseases – and certainly many pests – will only attack your plants in hot and rather dry conditions; so check from time to time that the atmosphere is moist enough for them. As with all things, prevention is better than cure. We suggest lots of ways, in the book, to give your plant the humidity it needs without having to live in a steam-bath atmosphere yourself. There is no need to invest in an expensive humidifying system, a saucer of

right way, properly fed – but when the room is dusted, the poor plants just don't get a look in. It's important to clean the leaves of your plant regularly. Here's why: in the presence of light a plant manufactures its own food in the leaves and green parts from water and nutrients taken up by the roots – a process called photosynthesis. If the leaves are covered in a thick layer of dust, then the light can't reach them properly. These leaves also breath and take in carbon dioxide to help make the food, so it is vital that the leaf pores don't get blocked with dirt and grease.

pebbles covered in water will do. Make sure you get the humidity right as some plants, the African Violet for instance, won't survive without it.

Cleanliness Counts, Too

Plenty of people appear to look after their plants impeccably – they're watered in just the

Settling In

Snatched from the nursery where they were raised and taken to unfamiliar surroundings where they experience changes of temperature and feeding, it is hardly surprising that newly bought plants can be in shock for a while. This is the time disease can strike and watering problems set in. So watch new arrivals extra carefully for the first weeks.

11

Leaf Tip Trouble

'My house plant has gone most peculiar, the very tips of the leaves have turned brown; it looks almost as if someone has tried to set light to them with a match.' Mrs. Y was a rather new house-plant owner. Until she had moved from a house with a garden into a block of flats she had never bothered to grow anything indoors.

'There are at least half a dozen things that could be happening to it to cause that look,' we told her. 'It depends on how you've been treating it. Pollution was often the cause, but now that people are more clean-air conscious and we have fewer open fires, and natural gas instead of coal gas, it's not likely to be that.'

'I know that most plants dislike central heating, that's why I thought this one would do well in my rather cold, draughty, mansion flat,' said Mrs. Y.

'The cold and the draught could well be the cause of the trouble,' we told her.

'But it gets plenty of sun and light because I keep it on the window-sill.' Mrs. Y told us.

'Even during that cold winter we have just had?' we asked her.

'Well, yes. .' Mrs. Y looked puzzled.

'The reason we're asking you,' we said, 'is that one of the commonest causes of brown leaf tips is scorching by the sun through the glass, but you can also get it in cold weather from frost damage. You see, if you leave the plant at night on the window-sill behind the curtains where it is cut off from the heat of the room, where the leaves touch the window-pane they can freeze if the temperature outside drops below zero. It's a thing that lots of plant owners forget. If this happens, the tips tend to curl up and die off. But the solution is simple: either move the plant into the room at night, or put a wad of newspaper between it and the glass to protect it.'

'I've got Venetian blinds, so it can't be frost,' said Mrs. Y. 'But it could be too much sun, particularly in the afternoons, as the window faces south-west.'

'It's as well to move it off that window-sill in any case,' we advised her. 'Just a foot away would do, or you could let down the blind when the sun is shining. Have you put a lot of fertiliser on the plant lately? This can cause browning problems. Another culprit is a fungus disease, but this shows itself as spots on the leaves, and these are two-tone rather than the dry, parched effect you describe.'

'I had no idea it could be so many different things,' said Mrs. Y.

'Oh, we haven't finished yet,' we said. 'It could also be overwatering, but, on balance, it is almost certainly the situation in which you've put the plant – too much burning sunlight, possibly draughts too, or frost. If you move it away from that window-sill, it should almost certainly recover its good looks.'

'Is there anything I *can* grow on a window-sill like that?' asked Mrs. Y. 'I'd like to have something there.'

'If there's really strong sunlight coming in, then cacti are the only things that could stand that direct heat without shade,' we said. 'But you could have geraniums and chrysanthemums on it in summer, and in winter bulbs would be fine.'

Leaf Spots

'I'm absolutely furious about this dracaena I bought a few weeks ago. I paid a great deal for it, but now I can see I've been given a diseased plant – it has gone all spotty!' Mrs. B sounded extremely indignant. 'With prices they ask for house plants these days, the least they ought to do is to give you value for money.'

'Troubles develop very quickly with house plants because of the warm atmosphere in which they live,' we said. 'So there is no reason to assume that the plant was diseased when you bought it. What kind of spots has the dracaena got?'.

Mrs. B sounded puzzled: 'Well . . just spots, really, darkish ones all over the leaves. It looks as though it has got measles.'

'There are several things that can cause spots on the leaves of house plants,' we told her. 'One of the simplest causes, for instance, is simply droplets of water left on the leaf's surface after you have been spraying it. These act just like magnifying glasses in hot bright sun and actually burn the surface of the leaf. However, as you say your plant looks as though it has the measles, the spots must be evenly distributed, so it's unlikely to be that. Neither is it likely to be the red spider mite which causes yellow speckling, since you say they are dark in colour. That leaves us with three possible causes. Are the spots like little dents in the leaves? With dark rings round the edges?'

Mrs. B went to have another look at her plant. 'No,' she told us. 'They're more like blisters.'

'Then it can't be Anthracnose', we said. 'We wondered at first if it might be. The way to tackle that particular trouble is to give the plant a good spray with a fungicide.'

'And where does your detective work get you now?' asked Mrs. B. 'I'm very worried the plant will die.'

'If the spots are crisp and dry, they could be caused by underwatering and overfeeding, but since few people combine the two, air pollution is usually the culprit. All sorts of things can affect house plants in this way – coal and paraffin fumes, for instance.'

'Well, these spots are almost wet looking. .' clearly Mrs. B was becoming rather impatient with us.

'Ah! Then this is a clear-cut case of a fungus disease which is actually called Leaf Spot.'

'Fungus! But I've done all the things I should do, I've kept the plant well damped down, it's almost like a steam-bath in there!' said Mrs. B indignantly.

'That's almost certainly the problem,' we told her. 'You see, too high humidity makes a marvellous breeding ground for fungi and bacteria. Move the plant to a light place that is drier, don't water it too much, cut off and burn any damaged leaves and give it a good spray with a fungicide. If the trouble comes back again, then dose it with a systemic fungicide which circulates in the sap of the plant.'

Pallid Leaves

Some people think that the so-called good tempered plants will put up with anything, and they don't have to bother too much about where they place them. Take the case of the pallid *Philodendron scandens*, or the Sweetheart Vine as it is so often called. It's almost a house weed, if there are such things, but even a philodendron can turn, as Miss P found out.

'I'm really disappointed about the way my cutting has gone,' she told us. 'A woman in the office gave me a piece of philodendron to grow on, and you'd imagine she'd handed over the crown jewels by the fuss she made about it. She's always asking me how it is. And now she's actually coming to a party at my flat

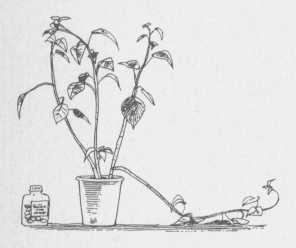

next week, and I'll have to hide the plant in a cupboard, or buy another one to replace it.'

'What's gone wrong?' we asked.

'Well,' said Miss P, 'it was started off in a jam-jar of water, then, when it rooted, I planted it in a pot, and it grew wonderfully for a time. I had visions of having a bathroom like a jungle, with plants trailing all over the place, but now the wretched thing has gone kind of

pale and spindly, and it's grown one-sided.'

'You say you're growing it in the bathroom, how dark is it in there?' we asked her. 'It sounds as though the philodendron has become drawn and spindly because it's trying desperately to reach the light.'

'I never thought of that,' Miss P sounded thoughtful. 'I suppose it is rather dark in there or, at least where the plant is, right in the corner. And come to think of it, it has one side right against the wall, so I suppose it couldn't really grow properly round the back.'

'Plants that are not getting enough light show it quickly by losing the colour from their leaves,' we told her. 'Fortunately it only takes a few days in reasonable sunlight to restore them to their former colour, but don't whisk a plant straight from deep shade into bright sun, do it gradually. It seems a shame that you are having trouble with your philodendron in the bathroom as this room, above all others, has just the right kind of moist atmosphere that house plants like. But perhaps you can find a spot a little nearer the window where it will thrive. Do remember, if you're keeping a plant against a wall to turn it at regular intervals, so that it keeps a good shape.'

'It does seem a shame that I can't use that spot for a plant,' Miss P persisted, 'isn't there anything that will do?'

'You could try something like ivy,' we suggested (see page 69 for some ideas on plants for dark places). 'But if it's so dark that the philodendron is unhappy, there's only one thing to do: install a small strip light there, keep it on several hours a day and grow a plant that way. Meanwhile move that philodendron somewhere else for a few days and by the time your friend sees it, it should be looking reasonably fit!'

Yellow Leaves

It happens to all of us: we commiserated with Mrs. D when she told us she'd bought a fine specimen plant, given it a lot of care and attention, then found it sickening. Its leaves had begun to yellow, and the plant generally looked unhealthy. 'What went wrong?' she asked.

'Well, the failure to form chlorophyll, the green colouring in plants, may be due to many different causes,' we told her. 'A lack of nutrients for instance. Other reasons could be root injury, or attacks by pests, and unfavourable conditions such as too high or too low temperatures. There are a lot of possible causes, but with a little thought it should be easy to eliminate most of them. The amount of light, warmth and water you give a house plant decides whether it will do well, or die. If there's not enough light, a plant will use more food staying alive than it will in producing leaves. It grows spindly, the leaves start to yellow. So, try putting the plant in more light, and make sure its leaves aren't totally shaded. Check the temperature, and see whether it seems to have enough humidity.'

'I don't think it's any of those things,' said Mrs. D, 'but I will check them out.'

'The first indication that all is not well with a plant is usually a drooping look combined with the yellowing of leaves,' we told her. 'This, in our experience, is nearly always the sign of a watering problem, and in most homes it is usually a case of overwatering. If it's only the older leaves that are yellowing and dropping, then it could well be underwatering. If the whole plant is affected then your suspicions will be reinforced by other signs, the leaf tips may go soggy and brown, for instance, or parts of the leaves may blacken and eventually drop off. If you look at the base of the pot and find signs of sogginess, then it's certain you've been lavishing too much water on it. Watch out, because root rot is only a short step ahead. If you're quite sure that the watering is correct, then it may well be that the plant needs feeding. A lack of nitrogen gives the plant a condition called chlorosis, and this may well be what's wrong. Are the leaves dropping rapidly?'

'No,' said Mrs. D. 'Some of them have dropped, but the rest are staying put although they're an awful colour.'

'If your tap-water has a lot of lime in it, that could also cause trouble, in this case you should dose it with sequestrene (iron chelate). As you've bought it recently, the soil should be of the right acid balance, so check out its minerals, and, if your tap water is really full of lime, a dose of sequestrene would help to get the leaves back to a healthy green.

Causes
Shortage of nutrients?
Overwatering?
Underwatering?
Too high a temperature?
Too low a temperature?
Bad light?
Lime in tap water?

Lower Leaf Drop

Old Mrs. A is a dear, fussing over her house plants like a hen with chicks, but she became worried recently when some of the lower leaves started to drop off her prize pilea.

'Don't worry too much,' we told her. 'Just one or two fallen leaves can indicate nothing more dramatic than the natural ageing process in a plant. All house plants at some time or other drop a few lower leaves as they make new growth. But it can, of course, be the first quiet warning that all may not be well. It could be a disorder that if unchecked may grow more serious and leave you with a denuded plant. So keep an eye on it, and at the same time check out any possible reasons for it.'

'It does seem as though rather a lot of leaves have come off,' Mrs. A sounded worried.

'If the plant has a waterlogged look about it, especially if water tends to lie, like a lake on top of the pot after you give it a drink, then overwatering could be the problem' we told her. 'And drastic action is needed (see page 21). But as you say only the lower leaves are dropping, then underwatering is much more likely to be the trouble.'

'It's funny you should say that,' said Mrs. A.

'I've never given it a lot of water, but recently I read in a book that it needs very little indeed, so since then I've only watered it about once a fortnight.'

'It's very difficult to say just how much water a plant needs,' we told her, 'Because it all depends on the living conditions – the hotter it is, the more you have to step up the moisture.'

'Well, as you know, we've had something of a heatwave lately,' said Mrs. A, 'that's when I cut down the water.'

'It does seem very likely, then, that you've probably not been giving it enough water,' we said. 'So keep it shaded for a little while, give it a good drink, and as soon as it shows signs of perking up, put it back in a lighter position. The only other reason we can think of for the leaves dropping like this is incorrect feeding, but as you're such an old hand at the house plant game, that's unlikely.'

'Well, fancy, and that's the first time I've read a book to find out what to do with my plants' said Mrs. A.

'You've obviously got green fingers, perhaps you should trust your instincts instead, in future!' we said to her.

Flower Bud Drop

There can be nothing more infuriating than to buy a nice-looking plant, covered with a mass of buds which promise weeks of delight when, within a few days, they all drop off! Mrs. T was harbouring dark thoughts about the garden centre which sold her the plant until we explained that very often a sudden drop of buds or flowers from a recent acquisition is simply the plant's reaction to a change in its environment. The shock of an instant move from the ideal climate of the nurseryman's greenhouse often disturbs it.

'Different light, or lower temperatures, can do this,' we told her, 'and remember how humid a greenhouse seems compared with an ordinary room. Then, if the plant has to cope with draughts too, buds are certain to drop off.

'We all like to put a new purchase in the sitting room, where it can be enjoyed when we relax and have time to look at it. But if this is in the less warm months and there's a fire going in the hearth, you have another reason for the plant's disapproval. Many flowering plants don't like coal fires or, come to that, coal gas fumes.

'If you'd had the plant some time before it began to drop its buds, then there could be other reasons,' we told Mrs T. 'First of all, check that its living conditions haven't altered, then think of other possible changes in its life. Camellias and gardenias, for example, shed buds when the temperature soars. You might also be giving it too much attention by overwatering, or even overfeeding. It needs food, but follow the instructions carefully on the packet, don't give too much. Only water the plant when it needs it, and that usually means when the compost looks and feels dry. If a peat-based compost has been used, scratch just below the surface to see, it may only have dried out on top. Underwatering is more rare – you usually know when that is the problem. But remember that the azalea is the exception to the rule, it needs more water than most plants (see page 36).

'I can't quite make up my mind which is the best place for this plant,' said Mrs. T.

'Well don't cart it around too much' we advised her. 'Flowering plants should be allowed to stay put. Don't take them to the sink to water them, bring the water to the pot, a budding plant doesn't like to be moved or turned.'

'What else causes bud drop?' asked Mrs. T.

'Well, the moist atmosphere that most house plants need to remain healthy is so often spoiled, today, by central heating or even air conditioning,' we said. 'Beat this by placing your budding plant on an 8-cm (3-in) layer of pebbles or gravel in water-filled saucers or trays. The pots must, of course, be kept above water level, but as the moisture evaporates it rises up around the plant and gives it the humidity it needs. The Christmas Cactus is a case in point: it must have humidity otherwise it will be infuriating and drop its buds just as you think they are coming into flower, all those gorgeous red or white blooms are lost. Apart from moisture, or the lack of it, the other thing that causes so much distress to a house plant is lack of light. If your window is not very big, it's well worthwhile placing a table lamp with a 100-watt bulb about 60 cm (2 ft) away from the plant. Leave the light on until about ten at night to give the plant a boost.

No Flowers!

'I definitely haven't got green fingers because nothing I grow ever seems to flower,' Miss H sounded quite disconsolate. 'I do like to have lots of flowers growing around me, rather than just foliage plants, but I've tried all sorts, and they seem very reluctant to actually come into bloom.'

'What kinds of plants have you chosen?' we asked her.

'Well, I started off with the Christmas Cactus,' said Miss H. 'It seemed to be going well, but no flowers appeared although I gave it plenty of light and kept it in a nice warm room.'

'You had a rather tricky plant there,' we told her, 'because it is one of a small group which needs just the opposite – rather cool conditions and not too many hours of light if you want it to put on a good show. Two similar kinds of plants are chrysanthemums and poinsettias; to get them going you must keep them fairly cool, with a temperature below 10°C (50°F) and restrict the length of daylight to a typical winter's day (page 35). Other plants react in the opposite way – you won't get flowers on most bromeliads, for instance, or fuchsias, and many annuals just won't perform unless they have at least twelve to sixteen hours of daylight.'

'How on earth am I supposed to know what to do, then?' Miss H sounded puzzled.

'Find out all you can about the plant's pedigree and habits when you buy it,' we told her. 'And remember that flowering plants are always more trouble to raise than foliage ones, so it might suit you better to go in for coloured foliage instead.'

'No, I'd rather stick with flowers, but I'll choose an easier kind next time,' said Miss H.

'You can still lose out on flowers from a number of different causes,' we told her. 'Lack of calcium in the soil – in other words, some garden soil that is too acid for the average house plant, could cause lack of flowers, so if you do put garden soil in a pot, make sure it is not too acid. Azaleas love it that way, but most other flowering plants object. Overfeeding a plant with fertiliser will encourage it to develop luscious green leaves instead of flowers. On the other hand, not feeding it will stop flowers from developing at all if it is in poor soil. In this case, giving a small dose of bonemeal will help it along. Gardenias and camellias, both lovely showy house plants to grow, hate too high a temperature and won't flower if they're kept in a room that's too hot.'

'Oh dear,' sighed Miss H. 'It all sounds very complicated.'

'As we said, flowering plants are more difficult to keep, but they're very worthwhile, you must just think of them as rather highly-bred pets,' we told her. 'Take achimenes, the Hot-water Plant, or Magic Plant as some people call it. It used to be a rarity you only grew in a hothouse. This one will sulk, and refuse to flower properly unless you keep it well watered – but you can hoodwink it into coming into bloom early after its winter rest if you plunge its rhizome (the strange stem that acts as a root) into hot water in early spring before repotting it. African violets and chrysanthemums can also be petulant about flowering once they've come into bud. But it helps them to get going if you withhold water and let the soil dry out a little. As you can see, all plants have personalities, it's just a case of understanding your particular specimen and getting it right.'

Wilt

'Oh dear, I've done something terrible to my begonia, it's wilting.' Mrs. N sounded really distressed. 'I'm rather new to house plants, you see, so I haven't the least idea what's gone wrong. It seemed all right at first.'

'A plant that wilts is telling you only too clearly that its leaves need more water than they are getting,' we told her. 'Do you think you have been keeping it too dry? Take a look at the soil in the pot, has it shrunk away from the sides like a cake does when it is cooked? Take a look at the leaves, too, could they be a darker green than normal? If that is so, it's a clear case that the plant hasn't been getting enough to drink and, in an emergency, the best first aid for this condition is to plunge the pot into warm – but only just warm – water for about a minute, and then leave it to drain.'

'It's definitely not too dry,' Mrs. N told us. 'In fact it could be the reverse I suppose. You see I realised about a week back that I must be overwatering the plant and I've cut down ever since. It did seem to pick up again, but now, like I said, it's definitely wilting.'

'It can't be a case of root rot, thank heavens, or the plant would have keeled over by now,' we said. 'You're lucky, because begonias are particularly tender in that way, and you have to be careful. How does it behave when you water it, what kind of soil do you have in the pot – a special potting compost or just something from the garden?'

'Oh, just something from the garden,' Mrs. N replied. 'It came from the shop in a small pot of compost, but when I repotted it I just added some earth from one of the flower beds. I tell you what, though, when I do water it now the water doesn't run away properly. It just lies on the top of the soil.'

'What's happened, in our opinion, is that you've got compacted soil there,' we said. 'This happens especially when garden soil is used instead of proper compost. It's been flooded at some time – probably when you overwatered – so the air-spaces between the particles of earth have been crushed down, and there's not enough oxygen left to keep the roots in a healthy condition. There's only one thing to do, take the plant out of its pot, scrape off as much soil as you can without damaging the roots, then repot it in a mix that contains peat or some other organic substance. Water the plant carefully, spray the leaves too, and it should recover. Remember, too, that begonias don't like direct sun. Watch out for another problem in future: a sudden rise in temperature can also cause a house plant to wilt, but we are sure, from what you say, that in this case the reason must be compacted soil in the pot.'

Possible Causes
Under- or overwatering.
Too much/too little fertiliser.
Poor drainage.
Hot sun.
Low humidity.
In need of repotting.

Slow Growth

'I'm really disappointed in the house plant that I was given for my birthday, it seems almost to have stopped growing, though it looks healthy enough'. Miss S has rung us from Newcastle about the Kangaroo Vine (*Cissus antarctica*) she's been given to brighten up her new bed-sitter.

'Do you know if it was bought from a shop?' we asked her. 'Because one of the reasons for a slow-growing plant is that it may have been put into the wrong kind of soil for its type, but professionally grown plants don't usually suffer in this way.'

'It was bought from a florist's in town' said Miss S. 'I know that because I saw the wrapping paper.'

'Well, then' we said. 'We'll have to look for some other reason. It could have been that it was taking a rest, you can't expect all house plants to go on merrily through the year growing at the same rate, any more than plants in your garden do. However, your vine rests in winter, so that can't be the reason, it should be making good progress at this time.'

'What do you think is the matter?' asked Miss S. 'I feel really fed up about it, it was doing so well, I'm training it up a stick.'

'Well, let's take a look at some of the other possible causes of the trouble,' we said. 'Do you think you could have been overwatering it? No? Then do its leaves seem shiny and good-looking? If they appear to be dull and lack-lustre, it might be that it is not getting enough humidity in the atmosphere.'

'Well, I haven't got central heating, or anything, in fact my room is rather chilly,' said Miss S. 'And it's rather gloomy, too, that's why I was so glad to get this plant, it cheers it up.'

'Those very factors are probably something to do with the fact that your plant seems to be doing badly,' we told her. 'The Kangaroo Vine doesn't want full sunlight by any means, but it does need some light, perhaps you are keeping it too far away from the window. But you can get round that by giving it a boost with artificial light. Does it look pale and drawn at all? It should be all right on temperature for it only needs 10 to 13°C (50 to 55°F) by day.'

'It's certainly not pale,' said Miss S. 'It's quite nice and green.'

'Could it possibly have outgrown its pot?' we asked her.

'I'll go and have a look.' Miss S sounded as though she thought we'd found the real cause of the trouble. 'Yes, it's practically toppling over.'

'Take a look at the bottom of the pot' we said, 'and see if there are any roots poking through. Tip the plant out carefully and see if there is a jungle of roots inside. It sounds to us as though it's a combination of several things – too small a pot, too little light and even possibly too low a temperature if the room is really cold. Put those right, and we're sure your plant will forge ahead.'

Slow Growth *Check List*

Temperature: too cool?
Light: too little?
Is it resting?
Does it need repotting?

Collapse

'Something awful has happened, one of my house plants has completely collapsed!' Mrs. C, who had only recently started growing plants indoors, sounded thoroughly alarmed. 'It's a begonia, and it was doing absolutely splendidly until last night, when I went to look at it and found it had keeled over. Now, and I don't know if it's my imagination or not, some of the others look the same. It's very embarrassing because my mother-in-law has come to live with us, and my plants have never had such devoted attention, she waters them every single day.'

'Then that's probably the cause of the trouble,' we told her. 'Collapse of this kind can be due to one of two things: under- or overwatering, and in your case it must be the latter. In fact, the commonest reason for all house plants dying off is root rot. Water left lying in the soil fills up all the air spaces and the roots can't breathe.'

'I didn't know they needed oxygen,' Mrs. C sounded surprised.

'They certainly do,' we told her. 'You can easily check if your plant has been affected: see if the soil is too wet – it should be like a wrung-out face flannel – and shake the pot gently to see if the plant seems unsteady. If it is, then almost certainly its roots are now almost non-existent.'

'What on earth can I do then?' Mrs. C was clearly worried.

'You can try some quick first aid,' we told her. 'Stir the soil with a kitchen fork to get some air in it, and put the plant in a warmer place to dry out. If the soil is really waterlogged you could ease the plant out of the pot for a while, then, once it has dried out, cut off any dead or injured pieces and put it in a cooler room and leave it for about ten days without watering. If the leaves look unhappy, spray them with a mister. After ten days, turn the plant out carefully to see if there's any sign of new roots – little whitish fingers at the base. Once new roots appear you can start watering again, but sparingly, please. And remember that a good watering once a week is much better than a little every day – tell your mother-in-law that, as tactfully as you can! If the soil is allowed to dry out between each watering, the plant's roots will grow longer to seek out moisture, and the plant really thrives.'

'Any other points to remember?' Mrs. C sounded more cheerful.

'Well, never stand a plant pot in a saucer of water,' we told her. 'And if you really want to pamper your plants, get into the habit of filling up a jug or watering can overnight with water (preferably rainwater) before using it. This allows the water to come up to room temperature and plants prefer it that way. Remember, too, clay pots dry out faster than plastic ones, and keep an eye on your mother-in-law's activities; if she persists in overwatering, buy her one of those special meters to show how damp the soil is for her birthday.'

Prescription for overwatering

Stir soil with fork.
Put plant in warmer room.
Allow to dry for 10 days.
When new roots appear, water cautiously.

Mildew and Botrytis

It's amazing how many people, who would recognise mildew quite clearly on their walls, somehow seem to miss it when it appears on their plants. Perhaps it's because it seems a rather unexpected thing to have on something green and alive. Anyway, when Mrs. O rang us about the strange blobs on the leaves of her new miniature rose, we realised after a moment or two what it was.

'It's powdery mildew,' we told her. 'If, as you say, it looks like blobs of flour on the leaves. There are two main kinds of mildew, the powdery mildew which we've just described and downy mildew, which is greyer and furrier, easier to recognise in fact, but more usual on outdoor plants like lettuces. Mildew is really a parasitic fungus, and its cause is usually damp in some form or other, though overcrowding can encourage it too, for the same basic reason. The plants, huddled too close together with their leaves entwined, give off a lot of moisture into the air which gets trapped between the stems and leaves, then, particularly if the temperature soars and conditions are right, mildew will break out. Roses are one of the worst victims, chrysanthemums, although they look so tough, are often affected too.'

'I think I know the reason, then,' said Mrs. O. 'You see, I went away for a few days and left the rose crowded with a lot of other plants on a piece of matting in the bath, so they could have a kind of self-watering system of their own.'

'The idea is fine, in principle,' we told her. 'But if you do that, you must make sure that there is plenty of ventilation. This problem is also caused by overwatering, perhaps you left them in too much moisture. But it's likely to be because the air wasn't circulating enough.'

'Do I have to throw the plant away? And do you think the others are affected?' asked Mrs. O.

'It's quite likely that the trouble may have spread without you noticing it,' we told Mrs. O. 'Miniature roses, in particular, are rather delicate to grow, and show signs of trouble rather quickly, so action is needed now. Cut out the worst affected leaves and stem tips and spray the plant with a fungicide like dinocap or benomyl (which the rose will take up into its sap), this is good against other problems with roses, black spot disease for instance.

'Botrytis is another fungus disease which may be a problem in bottle gardens and terrariums once it gets a hold, you'll often notice it on the surface of the soil first. Then the plants begin to look sickly and may well begin to die. This, again, is caused by overwatering, and the only choice here is to take everything out and start again with clean soil and new plants.'

Prescription

Reduce watering.
Reduce humidity.
Ensure good air circulation.
Cut off affected shoots and leaves.
Spray with dinocap.
Repeat spray with benomyl systemic fungicide.

Two-Tone Leaf Trouble

'I feel I've been cheated; this plant I bought at a flower show has lost all its stripes – do you think it's because it was grown by an amateur?' Mrs. K sounded extremely put out by the fact that the Wandering Jew, sometimes called *Zebrina pendula*, had lost its silvery tone and purplish stripes in some of the leaves since she acquired it.

'Striped or two-tone leaves – or variegated leaves to give them their proper title – are caused by a freak of nature,' we told her. 'In the case of plants like this, parts of the leaves are without chlorophyll, the green pigment which uses the energy from sunlight to convert carbon dioxide and water into sugar and gives the plant its food. This means that only part of the leaf is actually producing anything, and therefore many variegated plants grow more slowly and have to be treated with more care than ordinary ones. Zebrina and its cousin tradescantia are remarkably tough. They do, however, sometimes play up and lose their stripes. One of the main reasons is lack of light – variegated plants must have lots of light if they are to keep their stripes. But direct sunlight is not always good, ideally it needs to be bright but not too strong a light. Most striped plants will lose their variegations if they're put into deep shade.

'If you have a two-tone plant that seems to be reverting to green, take a look and see if it is getting spindly. Notice if, for instance, the leaves seem to be produced further away from each other on the stem, than they are nearer the base. Both of these factors are a sign that the plant is straining to reach the light. The zebrina, however, is a little different, we've found it needs a good warm temperature if it is to keep both its stripes and its pinkish tone. In colder weather it will tend to become greener than before. Remember, incidentally, that although we think of it as an indoor plant, it looks good in hanging baskets outdoors in summer.'

'Once the leaves have gone green, can they go back to stripes again?' asked Mrs. K.

'Very often on plants like tradescantia, the green is permanent,' we told her. 'But in the case of zebrina, the leaves seem to have the ability to switch to and fro. Certainly in the case of your plant, if you put it in the light and in the warm, it should become variegated again.'

'Does anything else affect striped leaves?' Mrs. K asked us.

'Well, overfeeding certainly has an effect,' we told her. 'Give a plant too much fertiliser and it busies itself, usually, making its leaves as green as it possibly can. In general, the thing to remember about all plants with variegated or coloured leaves is that with very few exceptions – and in this we would include the begonia – they need light if they are to keep their colour. If you put them somewhere warm and bright you shouldn't have any trouble in maintaining their variegation.'

Pests

The artificial, hothouse conditions we create to make house plants happy in our homes is also ideal for a whole host of uninvited pests. Aphids and mites, to say nothing of other nasties, tend to congregate on house plants in greater numbers, and more quickly than they attack things out of doors. The insects that, in their turn, prey on the pests – ladybirds for instance – are unlikely to find their way into the house, so the hapless plants suffer as wave upon wave of marauding insects zoom in.

How can we save them from pests? An eagle eye is the answer. Don't just water your plants, examine them carefully at every opportunity. Look, particularly, on the underside of the leaves where all sorts of things may be going on without you noticing them; a number of sucking insects, especially the red spider mite, lurk there. Fortunately we now have a battery of sprays and dips to kill them off, but best of all is the plant that is kept healthy all the time and doesn't need any of these.

Insecticides and fungicides are all, let's face it, lethal weapons to use; many of them are very poisonous indeed and should, literally, be handled with rubber gloves. Direct contact is not the only danger. If you are not careful you can inhale toxic fumes, particularly from aerosols. Children, dogs and cats must be kept well away from sprays, and don't forget the budgie or the goldfish. If you have one of the latter, take it outside not just until spraying is over but until you are quite sure that any fumes have settled.

The most efficient way to spray individual plants, both from the point of view of effectiveness and your own health is to stand the patient first in a large plastic bag – a rubbish sack is fine – then spray it carefully inside and close up the top quickly, leaving it like that for about an hour. Another method is to pop something – a cardboard box or a container like a waste-paper basket – over the plant immediately it has been done. This not only contains the spray, but makes sure that flying pests are unable to escape from the fumes.

Strike immediately: get your spray-can out the moment you see any sign of trouble. That way you'll keep things under control. Alternatively, if you don't feel happy using chemicals, soapy water or sometimes an alcohol like methylated spirits will often put paid to the pests just as well, provided they haven't got a real hold on the plant.

There are two basic kinds of killer chemicals to use – the straight insecticide which kills bugs off as it touches them, and the systemic insecticide. The latter works in a different way by being absorbed through the leaves and stem of the plant into its sap which becomes poisonous to the pest that sucks it up. Usually systemic pesticides are used as a preventive measure – if, for instance, other plants have been attacked, and you want to deter the insects from moving on. Contact chemicals like malathion, on the other hand, are used on pests which have already got a good hold, but never use this chemical on ferns and crassulas. It's often a good idea to start with a direct killer spray and follow up with a systemic one. But read the instructions on the cans carefully. It's vitally important, for instance, that you don't give your plant an overdose of malathion, or you could kill it just as surely as the pest. *Be sure, too that you buy a pesticide meant for indoor use, or you could be in trouble with poisonous fumes.*

Know Your Enemies

Let's take a look, now, at what we are fighting against on the pest front; the bugs that give your plants a sickly look.

Aphids are just about the most common house-plant pests. The two best known are greenfly and blackfly, these are tiny green or black insects which crowd together on stems, on the undersides of leaves and especially on the new young growing tips of plants. They feed by sucking the juice from the tender green leaves and shoots. Curled-under leaves which later become yellow and drop off are a sign of aphid attack. Almost all house plants can be affected by them but several of the showier kinds – cyclamen, begonia, chrysanthemum, gardenia and geranium – are particularly prone. A wash with warm soapy water will get rid of a minor infestation, but if drastic action has to be taken, reach for malathion.

Ants come in where there are aphids about, for they feed off the sticky secretions that aphids deposit on leaves. They have been known to kill off tiny seedlings too by digging around them and uprooting them. Tackle ants with one of the proprietary ant-killers or with malathion.

Whitefly are usually smaller than aphids, and are more often seen flying around – great white clouds of them fly up when a badly infected plant is touched. Marginally worse than the whiteflies themselves are the nymphs or scales, as the developing larvae are sometimes called. They appear like tiny seeds on the undersides of leaves from which they suck the sap and weaken the plant. Whitefly will attack almost anything in sight, they love the citrus, they're very happy on a coleus, a geranium and most annual flowering plants. Try the soapy water cure if you only have a minimum number to deal with, otherwise it's back to the malathion again.

Red spider mite isn't actually a spider, but it comes from the same family. It thrives in a hot dry place, so if you want to invite it into your home, turn up the heating, keep the humidity low. Mottled leaves or small yellowed patches are signs that the red spider mite is at work, but individual specimens are almost invisible. Citrus, ivy, hydrangea, poinsettias, philodendrons and African violets are all likely to become infested. Also coming under the heading of mites are broad mites and cyclamen mites which attack African violets as well. Use malathion for first aid, follow up with a systemic insecticide.

The rest of the gang that you're likely to meet up with in the average home, are *Scale insects* which have a real yen for plants with large leaves, the ferns for instance, and the *Mealy bugs* which make a plant deformed and yellow looking. Systemic insecticides are the only sure way of dealing with them if you want to get rid of the pests once and for all.

Prescription

Spray with malathion (not ferns), make sure you cover the undersides of leaves. For best results, leave a bag or box over the plant for a while. For long-term effect, spray the plant with a systemic insecticide which works its way into the sap and makes the plant poisonous to sap-sucking insects. Never use this on herbs, tomatoes or anything you are likely to eat.

'Cigarette Ash' On Leaves

'I don't smoke myself, but my husband does, and when I saw this greyish stuff over my citrus plant, I thought he had been flicking cigarette ash over it.' Mrs. X was particularly proud of the little lemon tree that she had grown from a pip, so she was naturally upset when the growing tips seemed to be dying back, and had what looked like grey dust on them.

'Are the leaves themselves grey in colour, or is there definitely something scattered on them?' we asked her. 'Leaves that seem to have turned grey can be caused by too much light, strange as it may seem. Some plants can actually get more sunlight than they need, especially if they come from shaded jungle conditions back home.'

'No, this is definitely a kind of dust,' she told us. 'I haven't looked at it all that closely but it seems like cigarette ash, or even snowflakes.'

'Then what you have is almost certainly a whitefly problem,' we told her. 'Whiteflies attack the plant by sucking the sap. Eventually the leaves get yellowish spots on them and they finally turn completely yellow and drop off. Have a look at the underside of the leaves, can you see anything on them?'

'Why, yes,' Mrs. X sounded surprised. 'There are some pale green things, almost like eggs, clinging to them. I never noticed them before.'

'Those are the nymphs, the embryo whiteflies,' we told her. 'You've definitely got an infestation there. Whitefly are particularly difficult to shift, so you must spray the plant and any others that might be infected.'

'Does this mean that I have to use an insecticide?' asked Mrs. X. 'Because I am really not very keen on them, I'd rather do without.'

'It really is the most reliable way to get rid of infestations like this,' we told her. 'Though mild attacks can be tackled by dousing the plant in tepid soapy water, in your case obviously something much more drastic is called for. You may also find that you have to follow up the first treatment with what we call a systemic insecticide, something that works through the sap.'

'I'll go out and get something right away, then,' said Mrs. X. 'Let's hope that it works, because I'd hate to lose the plant.'

'We're sure that it will,' we said. 'As long as you follow our instructions and spray the plant thoroughly.'

'I'll have to apologise to my husband!' said Mrs. X with relief.

Prescription

Spray with malathion, make sure you cover the undersides of leaves. For best results, leave a bag or box over the plant for a while. For long-term effect, spray the plant with a systemic insecticide which works its way into the sap and makes the plant poisonous to whitefly. Never use this on herbs, tomatoes or anything you are likely to eat.

Sticky Leaves

'I've been spraying a leaf-shiner on this tradescantia to give it a treat, but I must have overdone it, because the leaves have gone sticky.' Mrs. G produced a pot containing a plant that certainly looked sorry for itself.

'In the first place,' we told her, 'leaf-shiners, which are mainly a grooming product, are not meant for plants with soft small leaves like that. They're specifically designed to make large leathery leaved things like the rubber plant or the monstera look glossy and attractive. Now, let's have a look and see what's wrong.'

It was soon obvious that the shiner, itself, was not to blame for the plant's sorry state. The leaves were sticky, almost as if they'd been coated with honey – nothing like the waxy finish that a leaf-shine product gives. 'This is a clear case of honeydew,' we told her. 'It's a sticky substance that is secreted by one of three kinds of pests . . . scale insects, whiteflies or aphids. They all have one thing in common: they suck the sap of the plant and weaken it, so that eventually the leaves will turn yellow and drop off. This honeydew, as we call it, which they excrete, causes more trouble if it is allowed to remain, for it encourages the growth of an unpleasant fungus called sooty mould. As you would guess from its name, sooty black patches appear on the leaves which are very difficult indeed to get rid of. In fact the only way to fight back, on behalf of the plant, is to dose it with a systemic insecticide – that is a chemical which is absorbed into the sap of the plant.'

'How do I know which particular pest I'm plagued with?' asked Mrs. G.

'Whitefly are quite easy to identify because they tend to fly up in a white cloud around the leaves of the plant when you touch it,' we told her. 'Aphids can also be seen quite easily if you look carefully at the leaves. They're usually green, but you can get brownish-black or grey ones too. Scale insects are found most often on ferns, and they look rather different, almost like little brown limpets. The best way to deal with them is to attack them directly: wipe them off the leaves with a piece of cotton-wool soaked in soapy water.'

We picked up the plant and, sure enough, a very obvious shower of whitefly showed up. 'That's the commonest cause of sticky leaves,' we told her. 'But if the culprits had been aphids, the cure would have been the same – give the plant a good spray with malathion, making sure, by the way, that you get a plant spray specifically for indoor use, and, as it is very strong, please follow the instructions carefully.'

'What can I do about the sticky stuff on the leaves?' asked Mrs. G. 'It looks very unpleasant there.'

'Once the plant has been thoroughly sprayed and you've got rid of the whitefly,' we told her, 'it's a good idea to sponge the leaves individually with tepid water to which a tiny drop of detergent has been added. Then rinse them carefully with clean water at room temperature. Continue to keep a good watch out for whitefly, and aphids too, because tradescantia is a favourite with them. And remember that once you get these pests into the house, they are more than likely to spread to other plants.'

Cobwebby Plants

'Do spider plants actually attract spiders? The one I've got growing on my office windowsill has begun to look sickly and, what's more, it has got tiny cobwebs on it now.' Miss V had thought, when she took a plant from her flat into the warmer, heated atmosphere of the office, that it would do well. But, as so often happens, the reverse was the case.

'Are you sure there aren't any spiders on it?' we asked her. 'Cobwebs of this kind are almost certainly the work of a minute creature called the red spider mite, which sucks the sap out of the leaves making them look mottled. Then they eventually die. If you look very carefully indeed, you will probably find a fine red dust on the underside of the leaves. Rub them and you'll get a red tinge on your fingers. Red spider mites usually only appear in hot, dry atmospheres, that's why you had this problem when you moved your plant into just those conditions in the office.'

'What can I do to get rid of this mite?' said Miss V. 'I'm really very worried that if I take my plant back to the flat, the mites will attack my other house plants.'

'That is a risk,' we agreed. 'So perhaps it's best to treat it before you move it. Give it a good spray with malathion, make sure you coat the undersides of the leaves as well as the top. To make it more effective, it's a good idea to pop a cardboard box or a plastic bag over the plant immediately after you have used the spray. This contains it, and makes it work more thoroughly. Repeat the spray treatment at fortnightly intervals for the time being. And, by the way, do read the instructions carefully, you could kill off the plant if you use too much. If malathion doesn't work, then a systemic insecticide should do the trick, but this, too, is extremely poisonous to use. Liquid derris is another choice if the plant is not too badly affected and this also helps to increase the humidity.'

'I don't really like using chemicals,' said Miss V. 'Isn't there any alternative?'

'Plunging the plant in a bath of tepid soapy water sometimes gets rid of these little pests,' we told her.

'In commercial circles, however, where they get infestations – in greenhouses growing tomatoes and cucumbers for instance – they're using a new, non-poisonous, natural way to get rid of the mites by introducing a colony of *Phytoseiulus persimilis*, a tiny predator which feeds off the mites. But the trouble about using this creature in the home is that it has to have a supply of mites to survive, so that rather cancels out the benefit on a small scale! No, malathion should get rid of the mites for you. After that, keep your plant in a more humid, cooler atmosphere and you'll be all right. Greenhouses are the most difficult spots to keep mite free. The house plants to watch on the red spider front are the ivies, fuchsia, hydrangeas and the dracaenas. They tend to attack citrus plants too.'

Prescription

Remove from hot dry conditions.
Spray thoroughly with malathion, a systemic insecticide or liquid derris. Repeat once a fortnight.

'Cotton Wool' On Leaves

'Take it out, at once!' we shouted, as Mrs. W came in through the door, carrying her favourite African Violet plant. She'd been loudly explaining that it had some strange-looking cotton-wool blobs on its leaves, and what should she do about it? 'Take it away from our plants, for a start!' we said. 'That plant is infested with mealy bug, which is one of the most difficult afflictions to get rid of. You can spend long hours picking off these insects so we don't want them on our favourites.'

Mrs. W looked a little plaintive. 'Don't tell me that I will have to get rid of my plant. You know how difficult it can be to grow African violets, and I really work hard to give my plants ideal conditions.'

'Well, that's one of the problems,' we said. 'Sometimes, the better the environment for growing, the more the bugs seem to thrive. If your plant is being properly cared for, and it starts to wilt, look for a cause right away. If you get into the habit of really closely examining a plant each time you water it, or even as you pass it during the day, you'll soon learn to notice anything wrong.

'Mealy bugs are small greyish-white insects, and they make their presence known by the little blobs, exactly like cotton-wool, as you've noticed. These are usually tucked into leaf axils and leaves. They live by sucking sap from plant tissues so that, eventually, the plant develops sickly and undersized foliage. The leaves drop off, and the plant collapses and dies. Mealy bugs are very persistent, and if you find them in crevices, they are almost impossible to kill off completely. The African Violet, sad to say, is a favourite victim, as are the cacti. Let's hope they haven't got too great a hold in your case. If you move quickly, before they become established, then it should be possible to get rid of them. It's vital to do so because they bring other troubles in their train: they exude a 'honeydew' which attracts ants, and provides an ideal breeding ground for fungus as well.' We took a look at Mrs. W's plant. There didn't seem to be much infestation. 'You seem to have discovered it early,' we said. 'That's lucky. They breed at a very fast rate. Maybe you'll save the plant.' We told her to pick off the bugs one by one with a fine paintbrush dipped in methylated spirits.

'Then wash the plant with warm soapy water,' we said. 'Afterwards rinse it with clear. Then spray it with a systemic insecticide, which will be absorbed into the sap, and do this once a week for three weeks. Or spray with malathion. But keep picking off any bugs you see, and, in the meantime, keep the African Violet in quarantine, well away from other plants.'

Prescription

Pick off mealy bugs with a fine paintbrush dipped in methylated spirits.
Wash with soapy water and then clean water.
Spray weekly for 3 weeks with a systemic insecticide.
Or spray with malathion.

29

Other Nasties

A lot of house plants really enjoy a spell out of doors in summer, like Mr. T's fuchsia which was enjoying a summer holiday in a semi-shaded spot in the garden. 'It should be nice and cool there during the day,' we commented. 'Just right. Did you have it indoors during the winter?'

'Yes, and it hasn't suffered at all from the move, it's very good tempered.' he said.

'When you do move it back into the house before the first frosts, do make sure it hasn't brought any unwelcome visitors in,' we warned him. 'A pot that has been left half-buried in a flower border during the summer may well be the temporary home of an earthworm. Good friends though these creatures may be to the gardener outside, their activity inside a house-plant pot is too much by half. They will dig tunnels, making the root ball dry out quickly, and they can cause a lot of root damage.

Small slugs, too, can be brought into the house, having tunnelled themselves into daffodil or tulip bulbs you're planning to force for winter flowers. The way to cope with these pests on such a small scale is simple – just pick them off.'

'What other things am I likely to find on plants set out in the garden?' asked Mr. T. 'I've got a lot of things out at the moment including begonias.'

'They, like saxifrages and primulas, are sitting targets for the vine weevil,' we said. 'And that's something more difficult to deal with. The weevil's small fat white grubs live in the soil, and enjoy a good meal of roots, tubers or corms. A good dusting with BHC (gamma HCH) is the answer in that case.'

'Are caterpillars any trouble,' asked Mr. T. 'I've seen a lot of them around.'

'Caterpillars brought in from the garden hide in the soil at the top of the pot.' we told him. 'They'll come out at night to chew leaves, buds and flowers. It has been known for an entire plant to be stripped completely by them overnight. But, because of their life cycle, it's a problem you are more likely to encounter now, rather than when you bring the plants back indoors. The answer is to spray with malathion or derris to get rid of them. Earwigs often come into the house on cut flowers, especially dahlias, and they will emerge at night on the look-out for a meal: unfortunately your favourite house plant could well be on the menu! The young ones will eat fresh shoots, while the older earwigs are prepared to eat leaves, flowers, anything. Dust affected plants with BHC (gamma HCH) to get rid of them.

'Leafhoppers are pests which, indoors and outdoors, like pelargoniums and primulas. They appear as coarse white flecks on the leaves during the summer months out of doors, but any time of year inside. Spray them with malathion every couple of weeks to get rid of them. And, of course, the most common of all pests which the ordinary house plant will pick up in the garden in summer is the aphid. The remedy once again, is to spray thoroughly with malathion or derris.'

Thrips

'I've been through all the books on house plants that I've got, and I still can't find out what this plant is being attacked by,' said John H. His avocado plant did look sorry for itself. 'I've grown it from a pip, and because of our severe winters, that means a *lot* of care,' he added. The tips of the plant's new leaves were tightly curled. There was a whitish or silvery mottling on the older leaves.

'We've got a magnifying glass in the car,' we said. 'We'll take a closer look at the avocado's leaves through that.' And, sure enough, when we started examining the crevices of the plant, we could see some darkish coloured, flea-like insects. They were scurrying to find somewhere to hide when we disturbed them. They were visible to the naked eye, but only just.

'They're thrips,' we told John. 'They're not too serious fortunately, but they're not very common. It's particularly unusual in your case, but some people would say that if you got them on a bought house plant, you weren't being choosy enough when buying it. It's amazing that so many people just go out and hand over hard-earned money when purchasing house plants. Be what Americans call 'tyre kickers'. Do take a long, careful look before taking the plant away. If you buy a new plant with a bug in it, it might well infect other quite healthy specimens you've been nurturing.

'Thrips lay their eggs in the leaves or young stems of plants. The larva lives on the plant's tissues, literally sucking away its juices. Because thrips are relatively unusual, you should think of other pests first, if you're analysing trouble. But if you are watchful for the first signs of pest attack, you will see the yellowing of a section of a leaf or distortion of the growing point of the plant, which will show all is not well. Then you'll notice papery scars on the leaves, caused when the insect's mouth scrapes and scars their undersides. The whole leaf's surface becomes whitened and stippled. Mild attacks can easily be controlled by washing the plant with warm, soapy water, then spray with BHC (gamma HCH), malathion, or derris at weekly intervals until the thrips disappear.'

We were able to allay John's fears about losing the avocado. If plants are kept generally healthy, they're unlikely to die from minor attacks from pests alone. If the plant is neglected, and the pest gets the upper hand, then that's a different story. But it can happen, sometimes, that the insect is carrying a virus which it injects into the plant's sap, and in this case pale or mottled leaves and stunted growth indicate that the plant is suffering rather badly. If this happens, it's time to be tough – the only answer is to burn it.

Prescription

Mild infestations – use soapy water. For more serious outbreaks – spray with malathion at weekly intervals.

Particular- and Sometimes Problem-Plants

You could say that there is no such thing as a problem plant, rather it is a case of a perfectly normal plant being grown in problem conditions. For in their natural habitat some of the plants we admire so much and pay so much for are nothing more than weeds. Others are a different story and highly bred, like a pedigree animal, they may be difficult to cope with. All, of course, are totally dependent on us for food and water, and, above all, *when* and how they are watered. For pets, at least, can usually take a drink when they want to, whereas plants are force-fed.

Some plants quite unfairly have a reputation for being 'difficult', but more often than not it's simply the case that they need different treatment from the rest. Once you know how, they're perfectly amenable. Some plants seem to get on best with some people and die in the hands of others. The African Violet is one case in point: either you become an enthusiast, or you give up in despair. Yet the answer may lie in some quite small thing – incorrect watering, for instance, or trying to raise it in dry conditions. Given a second chance, you might find it flourishes for you.

We've taken a selection of plants which we've found from experience do seem to be labelled 'difficult'. Yet two at least of them – the Rubber Plant and the Swiss Cheese Plant – are among the most long-suffering, obliging pieces of plant furniture you could hope to own. It is simply a matter of finding out their particular preferences and sticking to them. Poinsettias, too, have a bad reputation and are often tossed on the compost heap at the end of their flowering season when they could, with a little skill, be made to bloom again the following year. Azaleas have been known to play up, but that is usually the fault of wrong soil. Palms are also given a bad name but they are among the most even tempered of all plants and are good in difficult spots like offices.

We have included cacti and bromeliads on the list, not because they are difficult – indeed, cacti are probably the simplest plants of all to care for – but because people very often simply don't know how to handle them, and will therefore cause the death of a cactus with over attention, or kill off a bromeliad because they don't realise it has to be watered in a special way. Plants can't speak, alas, but they can tell you in their particular way what is wrong. What you have to do is to read the signs.

If you're starting from scratch on the house-plant scene, then it is best to pick your new pets from the list on page 75, the easy ones for beginners. But, with luck, as you get to know them, you will find that growing plants indoors can be a fascinating and almost a compulsive hobby. Some of the most interesting plants of all are surprisingly easy to grow. Succulents are very good tempered – sansevieria, the most placid house plant of them all, is a succulent, for instance. It's well worthwhile, if you are going for a special plant, to take the trouble to search out a specialist grower in the game. There are, for example, many nurseries that concentrate on fuchsias, and offer a list with an amazing number of varieties, shapes and colours, from trailers to dwarf bushy plants. Geraniums are another case in point, don't just choose the old standards like the scarlet Paul Crampel which is really meant for bedding, go to a specialist nursery and you'll find a selection you've never dreamed could exist, and the same goes for African violets. Don't forget, too, that there are societies which help you swap news and views if you find yourself specialising in one favourite kind of plant. The best place to find out about these, and about growers who can help you add to your collection, is through the pages of gardening magazines.

If you're feeling ambitious and would like to start a collection of really interesting plants,

then consider the miniature rose. This is gaining more popularity each year as true miniatures, some of which are only 20 cm (8 in) high, appear. But roses, which seem relatively easy to grow out of doors, could be rated as problem plants when they are grown inside. Like a highly bred miniature dog, the miniature rose needs tender loving care to succeed. It loves the sun and must stay in a south- or west-facing window, and you may have to resort to artificial lighting too. When it flowers it likes warmth, but when it sheds its leaves in winter it needs somewhere cool to rest. It hates dry air, so the humidity must be increased. Above all it must be fed: you can get away without giving fertiliser to a lot of plants, but not a rose. It will very obligingly stand draughts, however, which few house plants will do. The miniature rose a problem plant? I think we all agree it is that – but *so* worthwhile to grow!

Sickly Cyclamen

'Why have cyclamen got this reputation for being so hard to grow?' asked Mr. S. 'I was planning to give my neighbour one as a Christmas present because she has been so good to us, but my wife says they can die off.'

'Cyclamen have an undeserved label for being difficult, mainly because they are given away as presents, often to people who've never owned an indoor plant before,' we told him. 'In fact, they're easy enough to keep going though they do, of course, die off in the spring when their flowering season is over, and at that stage most people decide to throw them away. They've one great advantage over other indoor plants: they can stand the cold at night, so they are safe, for instance, to leave on a window-sill. And of course they give a marvellous splash of colour in the winter-time when it is needed. Cyclamen, in fact, should not be given too much warmth. What they need is a cool, even temperature and, above all, no draughts – that is what kills them off. They are also particularly prone to wilting when subjected to coal, paraffin, or any other sort of fumes. As long as your neighbour keeps her gift plant in a temperature around 15°C (60°F) and away from direct heat like radiators or fires, it should flower for many weeks. This is not a plant that should be allowed to stand in its pot in a saucer of water – that's another way over-eager owners tend to kill them. It also needs feeding about once a fortnight when it's in flower.

'Cyclamens, like poinsettias, are often abandoned at the end of the season. But with the price of plants now, and if there's space to spare, it is well worthwhile to keep them over the summer. As the flowers fade, pull the flower and stem from the corm, and in early spring start holding back the water, giving only a little about once a fortnight until the leaves die back and come loose. Don't let water settle on the corm or it may rot. Now store the pot, corm and all, in a cool spot out of doors. Come September you should find that new leaves are just peeping through. This is the time to repot the plant in good rich compost to help it regain its strength. Give it a slightly larger pot than last year, leave it outside, but water it well and often. When the first frost is likely, bring it indoors. Like African violets, cyclamen hate their leaves getting wet especially when they are in bloom, so water carefully. A soak in a bucket is one of the best ways, but do make sure you don't overdo things, for, once again like the violet, the roots are liable to rot.'

'What is the bug that's supposed to attack them? Someone told me they were prone to mites,' said Mr. S.

'Oh, you must mean the cyclamen mite,' we replied. 'Although it is given that name, it is just as likely to attack several other kinds of plants, including the African Violet. These mites can stop the plant flowering, or they can make the leaves stunted and shrivelled. The best way to tackle this is to use a systemic pesticide which makes the sap of the plant poisonous to mites who suck it. A once-weekly spray for, say, three weeks in a row, should cure the trouble. Do tell your neighbour to keep her cyclamen in her bedroom if she likes, for it is a good spot for these pretty plants. And do get her to try it a second year, it may not come up to the standard of the first year's flowers, but at least it's free!

Pallid Poinsettia

'Is there any way that I can keep my Poinsettia to flower another year?' Mrs. L was asking one of the most common questions that we had during the 'phone in. 'I tried once before,' she told us, 'but when it started growing again those lovely red flowers were missing.'

'Those are not the flowers,' we told her. 'It's a mistake lots of people make. The red part of a Poinsettia is actually a cluster of bracts, a modified kind of leaf. The flowers are small and yellow, and you'll find them in the centre of these bracts.'

'Well, whatever you call those red things,' said Mrs. L, 'they didn't come back again.'

'The secret of getting a Poinsettia, or *Euphorbia pulcherrima* to give it its proper name, to colour up is quite simple when you know how,' we told her. 'It's a case of keeping the plant away from artificial light.'

'Why's that?' Mrs. L sounded understandably puzzled.

'Different plants need different conditions in which to flower,' we told her. 'Fuchsias, for example, have to have long hours of daylight before they will come into bloom. Poinsettias are quite the opposite, they will only colour up when the daylight hours are short. Provided they are kept to natural winter daylight and treated in the proper way, they will reward you again next year with coloured bracts. The plant should be dried off after flowering by gradually withholding the water, and put where the air is fairly dry at a temperature of 10 to 15°C (50 to 60°F). Leave it like that until May and don't water it at all, then cut the stems back to about 15 cm (6 in) from soil level and take it out of its pot. Shake off as much of the old soil as you can, then repot it in fresh compost in a well-drained container which is just large enough to take the roots comfortably. Give it a good soak and put it somewhere with a slightly higher temperature. Water sparingly at first, increasing the amount when the first growth appears. Allow only three shoots to develop. You will find at this stage it begins to be too large for its pot, so repot it once more, doing this carefully so the roots are not disturbed. During the summer give the plant a little liquid fertiliser feed every fortnight. Then, early in August, prune it back, cut out any thin straggly growth and pinch off the growing tips of most of the shoots leaving just a few of the strongest ones to grow on. Unless the weather is bad it's safe to put your Poinsettia outside in a sheltered spot, but once autumn is on the way bring it indoors to a sunny, warm spot. This is the time to start the treatment which will bring it into bloom by withholding completely any artificial light, even a switch turned on temporarily can spoil things. A Poinsettia must get its beauty sleep in the dark, and it needs 14 hours a day. Within a couple of months it should start colouring up again.'

'How very tedious.' Clearly Mrs. L was going off the idea of poinsettias. 'And to think they are so popular as Christmas presents.'

'There is a way round the problem,' we told her. 'You simply get a large black plastic bag and pop it over the Poinsettia each night, just like putting a cover on a parrot's cage, but make sure it doesn't allow even a chink of light through by securing the bag round the pot with an elastic band. Have fun, and bring it into bloom at almost any time of year you want.'

Off-colour Azalea

'I've had a lot of success with azaleas in my garden, but this one, which a friend gave me to grow indoors, is playing up.' Mrs. J was clearly puzzled why that small and attractive shrub which looked after itself happily in the garden behaved in such a petulant way indoors.

'You say it was a gift,' we said. 'In that case it is probably the Indian azalea which is really a rhododendron hybrid and comes from Japan. These are often forced so that they bloom early and they can cause problems if you don't know how to deal with them.'

'Do you mean they are forced, like bulbs?' asked Mrs. J.

'Yes' we said. 'The process puts the plant under a certain amount of stress and it takes time to recover, but what is wrong with it?'

'Well, I've had it for a few weeks and it was fine at first,' said Mrs. J, 'then the flowers started to go brown and shrivel, some of the leaves dried up and began to fall off too.'

'It's underwatering that does that,' we told her. 'We know we're always saying overwatering is the main cause of plant troubles but there always has to be one exception to the rule, and in this case it's the azalea. It must have wet conditions in which to grow. If you let the soil dry out, even momentarily, it will sulk and shed its flowers and eventually its leaves too. It's difficult to get the watering just right for this pernickety plant but there is a clue to look for – examine a well-watered azalea carefully and you will see a tidemark on its main stem, just about 1 cm (½ in) above the soil level. This is where it should be, too low and the plant has been allowed to dry out, too high and you're flooding it. The best way to water an azalea is to give it a good bath by plunging the pot in a basin of water at room temperature. If you can make it rainwater so much the better, for your tap water may contain lime which azaleas hate. They must be kept in an acid soil.'

'But I can't go round collecting rainwater,' said Mrs. J, 'is there anything else I can do?'

'You can dose it occasionally with sequestrene – chelate of iron in other words. This chemical helps the roots to get the iron they need from the soil; lime, for some reason locks it in.'

'How will I know if it needs this stuff?' asked Mrs. J.

'Well, it will develop a condition called chlorosis,' we told her. 'The leaves will turn yellow between the veins which will stay dark green. It's very easy to spot.'

'Do all the leaves drop off, then?' she asked.

'Not if you treat it quickly,' we told her.

'What do I do when my azalea has finished flowering?' asked Mrs. J.

'Put it outside for the summer in a shady place,' we told her. 'It needs to be kept cool. Keep the roots moist, spray the plant regularly, then bring it indoors before frost is likely and it should start budding again.'

'Is it possible to keep it indoors, instead?' asked Mrs. J.

'Yes, as long as you choose a cool place,' we said, 'but keep it out of too much direct light. As soon as there are signs of fresh growth, bring it into warmer, lighter conditions and step up the watering, don't forget to keep an eye on that tidemark. There's just one more point, by the way, if you find that you have to repot your azalea at any time, do remember that you must use a lime-free compost, best of all one with some peat in it.'

Sad Solanum

'I'm determined to try and keep the berries on my Jerusalem Cherry this time,' said Mrs. Z. 'The one I bought last year seemed to drop them almost straight away.'

'The solanum has a bad reputation for doing this,' we told her, 'but it's usually due to one of three things. It likes bright conditions and it will sulk and drop its fruit if it doesn't have enough light. But, on the other hand, if you put it in very strong sunlight it will do precisely the same thing, lose its berries.'

'Well, it's not getting too much sun,' said Mrs. Z. 'If anything it is in too much shade, so perhaps I'd better find another home for it.'

'Well, don't put it anywhere where there is likely to be a draught,' we warned her, 'because that can be the cause of berry drop too. We're sure that if you check up on those three things, you will find that one of them is the cause, and it sounds to us as though you kept last year's one in too dark a spot. Some people believe, incidentally, that if you add a pinch of Epsom salts to the plant's water, every three weeks or so, that helps it to keep its berries longer – it's certainly well worth trying.'

'I've often wondered if you can keep these plants from one year to another,' said Mrs. Z. 'I threw last year's one away.'

'It's perfectly possible to hang on to a solanum after it has finished fruiting,' we told her. 'After all, it is a perennial plant. What you do is to cut the branches back by one-third in spring, leave it out of doors in a warmish spot all summer, and bring it indoors in the autumn before the frost. Given this treatment it should perk up again and start new flowers. But you can grow fresh plants from seed if you prefer.'

'I didn't know you could buy packets of seed for house plants,' said Mrs. Z.

'There are quite a number of kinds listed in the catalogues,' we told her, 'and the *Solanum pseudocapsicum*, to give it its right name, is one of them. But you could save the berries as they drop, and use the seeds from inside when the fleshy coat has shrivelled. Either way you need to start very early in spring. Sow the seed indoors, as early as February, and pot on the seedlings in the usual way. When the plants have grown to a reasonable height, pinch out the growing tips and, eventually, the side-shoots too, to keep the plants nice and bushy. Put them out of doors in a sheltered spot all summer, keep the soil just moist, and bring them in before the frosts. When the first starry white flowers appear, spray the plant daily with water to help pollination, or do the job yourself with a paintbrush – just dab it on one flower, and touch another with the pollen you've picked up.'

'It all sounds fairly easy,' said Mrs. Z. 'I might have a go at growing some to give away as Christmas presents.'

'Well, be careful not to give one to a family with small children,' we told her, 'because the berries are very poisonous. The solanum is basically easy to raise and look after. It appreciates an occasional spray, and it needs regular feeding. It will drop its leaves, though, if it has to cope with too high a temperature – 10°C (50°F) is about right.'

Bromeliads: The Pot-less Plants

Miss M rang us up and told us a girl friend of hers was moving, and wanted to give her one of her plants as a memento. 'Although it's nice to look at, it's growing out of a piece of wood. Is it a parasite? If it is, I don't think I like the idea of that in my flat,' she said.

'It's a bromeliad,' we told her, 'and we're sure you'll like it if you like pineapples, because they're the same family.'

We explained to Miss M that, in their natural state in the jungles of South America, these plants grow along the branches of trees. They don't take any nourishment from their hosts so they're not parasites. They root in decayed leaves and the other debris that col-

lects in crevices of bark and the forks of branches. Of course, in the home they can live in pots, but it's easy to make a nice display in a small log picked up from the countryside. Simply place a mix of sphagnum moss, peat and a leafmould – preferably from oak or birch – in a hollow in the log and let the plant root in that. Or you can line a hanging basket with cork, add a little of the mix, and the plant will thrive. They're beautiful to look at, and quite easy to grow as long as you give them as much sun as possible in the winter. In the summer, copying their natural environment, it's beneficial to filter the sunlight through a curtain. When you water, use soft water, and make certain that the 'vase' formed in the centre of the leaf rosette is kept filled. This is very important, because the inside of the leaves at the base are moisture-absorbing areas. The compost should also be kept moist, but not saturated.

After most bromeliads have flowered, they begin to fade. But they produce a number of offshoots before they die, each of which makes a separate plant. Leave them as long as possible on the mother, say until they are about half the size of the parent, before taking the old plant from its perch and removing the offshoots. Place them at first in very small pots of the special compost mix. As we told Miss M 'There's no problem growing bromeliads, one kind is reported to quite like growing on telegraph wires!'

Cactus Care

So many of us who now have houses full of exotic plants were lucky to be started off in the hobby as children, by the gift of a small hairy cactus from a school friend or a thoughtful relative. That is probably why people never seem to lose their affection for these undemanding plants.

'Why doesn't my cactus ever bear flowers?' Several of us were admiring a friend's collection of cacti and succulents when Mrs. R asked the question.

'It's more often than not to do with the watering,' we told her. 'If you want a cactus to have blossom then you have to withhold water completely throughout the winter, say from early autumn to early spring, and keep it in a cool temperature around 6 to 7°C (45°F). Under these conditions the plant bears flowers as in its natural state.'

Cacti and succulents are fascinating, we think of them as the cats of the plant world: enigmatic, but there's a lot going on! Cacti and succulents *do* differ, and it's important to know how because their needs are not the same. A succulent is any plant which stores in its fleshy stems or leaves considerable amounts of moisture so that it can withstand dry soil and arid air. And cacti, which store water in their stems only, are just one special branch of this giant family. You can tell the difference by the fact that cacti have hair or felting round the base of their spines – if there's no hair, then it's not a cactus. Succulents must have some water in winter – just enough to prevent them from shrivelling – but cacti must be allowed to dry out.

The needs of cacti and succulents are few but definite, and these are based on their natural environment where there's been plenty of light, a scarcity of water and a short growing season. In winter keep cacti dry, and in a temperature around 6 to 7°C (45°F); the spare bedroom is a good place. Succulents need just a minimum of water at this time. In summer cacti are at their happiest on a sunny window-sill while the rest of the succulent family can do with a little more shade.

After a dry winter, both kinds can do with a good drink in spring. Immerse the pots in tepid water until all the air bubbles cease to rise. Then drain them well and put them in a good light but avoid direct sunlight for a few days until their tender tissues get used to the change in the environment. During the summer growing season they like regular supplies of water, but do make sure the potting compost is well-drained. Use tepid water, never cold and straight from the tap. Above all, avoid overwatering – it's the cacti killer.

Palms and Ferns

'I'm moving into a new, very modern apartment and everyone says that I ought to buy some palms or ferns to decorate it, but I don't know anything about them. Are they difficult to grow?' Mr. G was the managing director of an engineering company and often entertained important customers at his bachelor flat.

'Palms do have an unfair reputation for being hard to keep going,' we told him, 'but this is mainly because they are used so much for display and, therefore, end up in showrooms and restaurants where they can be badly neglected.'

'What about the way the leaves often look ragged and brown round the edges,' asked Mr. G.

'Both palms and ferns drop their leaves from time to time,' we said, 'and, by a natural process, these will go brown first, that's when they should be taken off. But a palm or fern that goes brown at the edges is almost certainly being kept in too dry conditions. Palms kept in a draught can behave this way too.

'As specimen plants – and that's what both palms and ferns are – they stand out as a living work of art. They are amazingly easy to keep looking good, too, as long as you give them the one thing they really need – plenty of humidity. In fact, it's a good idea to put ferns under the shower occasionally to really drench their leaves, but make sure that the crowns at soil level dry out afterwards or they may rot.'

'What kind of plants should I buy?' asked Mr. G. 'To me, a palm tree is . . . well, a palm tree, and the same with a fern, but I'm told there are some very different types around. I do want something that looks like a real palm.'

'In that case, you're thinking of what we call the Concert Hall Palm,' we told him. 'Its official name is the Kentia palm, or *Howeia forsteriana*. It's amazingly tough, for as you can imagine it is often carted to and from concert halls and receptions. But it is also expensive to buy unless you are prepared to put up with a small plant. Another obliging pair of palms are *Cocos weddelliana*, the Coconut Palm, which is a slower grower, and *Chamaedorea elegans* (*Neanthe bella*), the Dwarf Mountain Palm, both of which are best for a small space. If you can provide lots of sun you could try the pigmy Date Palm, *Phoenix roebelenii*, which can reach up to 2.5 m (8 ft) and even give you flowers occasionally if you give it a rich soil and plenty of fertiliser. Palms like an acid soil, and in summer they need a good liquid feed. Don't repot them unless it's absolutely necessary, as they dislike change and their roots damage easily.'

'How do they differ from ferns?' asked Mr. G.

'Ferns must have humidity too,' we told him, 'but they can stand damp soil, which palms dislike. They must be drained, though, and appreciate being put on a saucer of moist gravel to help keep their roots cool. Ferns we would recommend for you are Hen and Chickens (*Asplenium bulbiferum*) which has that feathery look and produces plantlets on its leaves, or the Boston Fern (*Nephrolepis exaltata*) which is also called the Ladder Fern and which likes a warm humid atmosphere. There are dozens of other ferns to choose from, ranging from the tiny Maidenhair Fern, adiantum, to the weird Stag's-horn Fern (*Platycerium bifurcatum*).'

Fuchsias

'My grandmother grows marvellous fuchsias, but it's very embarrassing each time she gives me one for my own home as the wretched thing dies on me.' Mrs. E was a keen gardener, so failing with fuchsias must have been a particular annoyance to her.

'To start with you have to remember that they are basically outdoor plants,' we told her. 'We know this goes for all house plants but these really do appreciate the open air. It's hopeless to try and keep them going indoors during the hottest months, they must go outside in summer.'

'Perhaps that's where I've gone wrong,' said Mrs. E, 'but why do we grow them indoors at all for that matter?'

'Because the showiest ones are only half-hardy,' we told her, 'and the frost would kill them. There are some hardy ones but they are not nearly so spectacular. Fuchsias are also difficult about light – they must have plenty of it if they are to reward you with blooms, but, by the same token, they wilt in very hot sun and may need shading from it. It's light, rather than direct sunlight they want.'

'One of the main problems I've had is that the flowers come into bud, then drop off,' said Mrs. E.

'That's almost certainly a watering problem,' we told her. 'Both under- and overwatering produce these results in a fuchsia. The soil should be kept just moist during the flowering season, but in winter, when the plant rests, the soil must be left nearly dry.'

'It's mainly in spring that things seem to start going wrong,' said Mrs. E. 'Another thing I notice is that my plants look so untidy.'

'Fuchsias need careful pruning,' we told her. 'Not just for shape but for flowers too, as they flower on shoots made that year. You can prune in early spring, but to get them to give even better blooms, cut them back in the autumn, nipping off any shoots that were produced the previous summer. Next spring, when growth starts again, bring the plant into a warmer place and start watering again, sparingly at first. It's a good idea, too, to spray new shoots over with a mister containing clean water. In about six weeks you should have a good looking plant which will probably need repotting. This is about the time to give the plant a top-up with fertiliser.'

'I've seen some pretty standard fuchsias, are they difficult to grow?' asked Mrs. E. 'They cost such a lot in the shops.'

'It takes mainly patience and time,' we told her. 'First of all you encourage the centre stem to grow by taking off all the side-shoots from a young plant, but keeping the leaves that grow out from the stem directly. As the plant grows taller, tie the stem to a stake to encourage it to stay straight, and carry on taking off those side-shoots.

'Then, when your plant has reached the height you want, and by now it will be looking curiously lanky, you can let side-shoots develop at the top. By pinching these out at the tips when they are just a few inches long they will branch and grow more strongly. Eventually you will find a good bushy head has developed. Or you could grow a pyramid: let the main stem grow, pinch off the tip, prune the side-shoots so they widen as they go down. It looks attractive this way.'

African Violet Rot

'Well, I'll give it another chance,' we heard the middle-aged lady say, standing in front of a glorious display of African violets. 'I've had dozens of these plants because I like them so much, but I've never been at all successful. But I'll buy just one more because they are so lovely.'

The African Violet, or saintpaulia, is one of the most popular of all house plants. Some people find it easy to cultivate while others, like the middle-aged lady, can never rear them. Basically what is needed is a warm, shaded, humid position.

'Do you always put your plant in the same place?' we asked her.

'Yes, I've got a nice window-sill in the kitchen which has the sun all day long,' she told us. 'It needs it, because, after all it does come from Africa.'

Admittedly the plant does come from East Africa, but that doesn't mean it can cope with continuous direct sunlight. It likes the warmth though, and as long as the temperature doesn't drop below 18°C (65°F) it will brighten the home throughout the year.

'Most of my plants seem to have rotted,' said the lady.

'Well, without doubt, the main reason why people lose their African violets is from rot, caused by either overwatering or the wrong kind of watering,' we told her. 'The crown and the roots of the plant rot very easily, so if you swamp the soil with water and let it lie there, the roots will die off. And if you do the same thing from above, on the crown, that too will rot. Even splashes on the leaves can cause trouble. Water your saintpaulia from below, stand the pot in a saucer of tepid water, leave it for an hour and then pour any spare water away. To increase the humidity, stand the pot in moist peat or moss, putting several plants together if you can. Pinch out the flowers as they die off, otherwise they will rot. If the flowers are slow to come, keep the soil a little dry.'

African violets will appreciate a little extra artificial light from a table lamp in the evening. But if you want to give them a real treat occasionally, give each plant a steam bath. Stand it on a brick or upturned basin inside a larger bowl, pour in boiling water carefully to just below the bottom of the pot, and leave until the water cools. The plant will love it!

Rubber Plant Problems

The Rubber Plant, *Ficus elastica*, is probably the most popular of all house plants; it looks brave and fine with its glistening dark green leaves. As it seems to add a special quality to the decor of a room it is small wonder so many indoor gardeners find a place for it in their homes. But hardly a day goes by when we're not asked the familiar question: 'What's wrong with my Rubber Plant? Nearly all the leaves have dropped off.'

Overwatering, killing by kindness, sometimes overfeeding too are almost always the causes. The leaves of the Rubber Plant are thick, leathery and long lasting. It takes a lot to make them drop, so sadly it means considerable damage has already been done before they do, and the symptoms have become noticeable.

If overwatering seems to be the trouble, and it usually is, let the pot dry out for at least a week, then start watering sparingly again. Never, ever water the ficus in dribs and drabs, give it an occasional good soak instead. You will find it a most amiable plant to keep once you have the right conditions for it. It will grow quite well in a shady room, co-exist even with central heating, although it doesn't like to be too near a gas or electric fire. It doesn't like direct sunshine either, and grows best in indirect or filtered sunlight. It is happiest in temperatures around 15°C (60°F) and above with a high humidity.

To keep the Rubber Plant looking good, sponge the leaves once a week with tepid water to which a little milk has been added. Not only does this improve the plant's appearance, but it allows it to breathe more freely. Also, cleanliness is a protection against pests like scale, mealy bugs and red spider mite. Be careful with new leaves, they are protected by a red sheath which should be allowed to drop off naturally.

Newly-bought or repotted plants won't need feeding for six months. Only when the ficus is growing vigorously should feed be given, and it certainly won't need it in the winter. The Rubber Plant thrives in a small pot, and you can get a fine 1.25 m (4 ft) specimen growing in a 15 cm (6 in) pot. Don't be too anxious to repot, it does quite well in small containers. The plant will tell you when it has outgrown its home by a general lack of looks and stunted new leaves. Repot it in early spring using a general purpose potting mix.

General Care

Water moderately, keep soil barely moist at all times. In the winter reduce to minimum.
Feed only in growing season.
Keep away from gas and electric fires as well as draughts.
Wipe leaves with tepid water or water and milk, once a week.
Keep out of direct sunshine.

Moping Monstera

'My Swiss Cheese Plant has got no holes in it,' is one of the most frequent cries for help we get, and it seems that this, one of the best known house plants of all, doesn't always come up trumps. Known by several different names – the Mexican Breadfruit for one, the Split-leaf Philodendron for another (though this is more likely to be *Monstera pertusa* which looks similar but is smaller) – it is, in fact, easy to grow. Mrs. F was a typical caller, and she was particularly upset because she had noticed the leaf tips of her plant were going brown too.

'Let's start with the holes in the leaves,' we said. 'Is it a very young plant? Because you can't expect any slits in the leaves until there are at least three fully grown ones.'

'No, it's quite big, some of the leaves have holes in them, but the newer ones at the top of the stem are plain,' she said.

'Each new leaf, which starts off tightly wrapped, seems not to have any slits in it at first, but these appear as it unfolds,' we told her. 'But as you mention several leaves, there must be another reason. Light, or rather the lack of it, is one of the main factors behind unperforated leaves. Poorly split leaves, or no slits at all, can be caused by the plant being kept in too-dark conditions, although the monstera can usually stand a fairly dim spot. If you get very long stems with leaves stretching out towards the window, then it is probably in too dark a place.'

'No, it's got plenty of light,' said Mrs. F.

'In that case it probably needs repotting,' we told her. 'To encourage leaf slits and holes a monstera must have plenty of room to flex its underground roots, in fact it needs a pot larger than you would normally choose for that size.'

'I did wonder if it needed another pot,' said Mrs. F. 'Tell me, what are those tails hanging down from the stem?'

'They are aerial roots,' we told her. 'The monstera is really a climbing plant and it uses these roots to help it climb up trees. The best thing to do with them is to train them down into the pot or, better still, make a support for the plant from a cylinder of chicken-wire covered with moss and take the aerial roots into that. Once the plant gets very big with lots of these roots, it doesn't hurt to trim off one or two.'

'What about the brown edges on the leaves?' asked Mrs. F.

'That's almost certainly overwatering,' we told her. 'The monstera doesn't like too much water. The compost, which should be peaty, should feel like a wrung-out flannel. Let it almost dry out between watering. If you overwater a monstera it shows it by "weeping", producing droplets of water on the edges of the leaves.'

'Does it ever have flowers?' asked Mrs. F.

'Not until it is quite mature,' we told her. 'Then you could get a strange fruit too. Feed your plant in spring and summer, cut down the water in winter, keep it in a temperature which is never less than 13°C (55°F), and who knows, one day you may find yourself breakfasting off your own Mexican Breadfruit – they say that it tastes just like tropical fruit salad!'

Forcing Bulbs

'I want to have a go, this year, at forcing bulbs for flowers at Christmas,' said Mrs. L. 'Can you tell me how to do this? I like to see a touch of spring indoors when the world outside is dark and gloomy.'

'It's quite simple to do,' we told her. 'But if you definitely want flowers for Christmas, you will have to buy bulbs that have been specially prepared for this. These are treated by the grower so their normal growing cycle is advanced. They do this by harvesting the bulbs extra early, and then storing them for a special length of time under strict temperature control so they bloom ahead of their natural time. Some bulbs, hyacinths for example, are heat treated, while others like tulips are cold stored. You will have to pay extra for these bulbs but they do make sure you get your blooms on time.'

'When should I start, then?' asked Mrs. L.

'Hyacinths must be planted in their containers before the end of September,' we told her. 'Daffodils can wait until the second week of October, but tulips must go in in the first half of September to get them ready in time. If you are a beginner at the game, hyacinths are the easiest. Bulbs need a period of cold to develop properly. During this time they are busy developing a good root system before the stem and leaves really get going and need support. So we leave bulbs in their containers in the cold at first until about an inch of growth can be seen. Later they can be brought into the warm house, where they are literally forced into flower earlier than they would be in the garden. Make sure the bulbs are plump and solid and free from maggots. Choose a container at least twice their depth to give room for the roots to grow, and use a proper commercial potting compost for the job. Above all, make sure the container is drained properly.

'Partly fill the pot with compost and put the bulbs gently but firmly on top, so their tips are just below the level of the rim. Make sure they do not touch each other or the sides of the pot. Now add more compost, pressing it firmly with your fingers, and leave just the bulb tips sticking out. Water each container thoroughly and store them in the cold and dark. A cool frost-free cellar, garage or outdoor shed are fine, or you can leave them out of doors buried in ashes or sand. First, though, bag them up in black plastic to exclude the light. Once they've sprouted well, take them out of store, unwrap them and put them in a semi-dark area with the temperature below 15°C (60°F). Then, after a week, they can be placed in full light where they will bloom in a few weeks. The cooler the temperature they have, incidentally, the longer the flowers will last.'

'When should I bring them indoors?' asked Mrs. L.

'Well, for Christmas flowering, bring hyacinths indoors about December 5th,' we told her. 'Daffodils and tulips should be brought in on the first day of December to get them into bloom in time.'

'Do I have to throw the bulbs away afterwards?' asked Mrs. L.

'No, that's a mistake many people make,' we told her. 'Although you couldn't bring them indoors and force them again, plant them out in the garden in the autumn, and the following spring they should produce a pretty display of flowers.'

Planting and General Care

Some plants are very easy to grow, in fact they almost look after themselves – turn to page 75 for our personal list – others are like prima donnas and drive their owners to despair. All plants, however, benefit from good regular care, and it is amazing how they react to a change in their routine. We parked a coleus of ours with another house-plant enthusiast for a fortnight recently, and when we got it back it had gone almost bald. What caused this? A change in environment most likely, certainly not lack of attention. Perhaps the plant pined, we don't know, but back in its usual spot it has started to grow foliage again.

Have everything going for your plants. Start the right way by making sure they have well-drained pots to live in with the correct potting compost. Clay pots *must* have a layer of broken crocks over the hole in the bottom or you will have drainage problems. This is unnecessary with plastic ones which usually have several small drainage holes in them. Make sure the compost is right; it's lunacy to use ordinary, bug-ridden garden soil, so don't be tempted. There are two kinds of compost to choose from, proprietary loam-based ones like John Innes No. 1 (for seeds and young plants), No. 2 (for grown plants) and No. 3 (for extra large plants); or you can use a loam-less type, usually a mix containing peat. This is lighter and drains well but needs watching for it dries out very quickly in hot or sunny conditions. It can be unwise to mix the two, for they need differing amounts of water.

Watering, once again

While on the subject of water, we can't resist ramming home the lesson once again: don't water your plants on the little-and-often principle. Water that barely goes below the surface of the compost, as frequently happens in this case, encourages the plant to grow fine hair roots high up, instead of where you want them, down below.

. . and Cleaning

Do keep the leaves clean, wash them regularly with tepid water and, if they seem to have grease on them, add just a drop of soap or detergent. Only use leaf-shiner on plants with thick dark leaves, and then use it sparingly and never in low temperatures.

Plants without soil

A new word has cropped up on the house plant scene – Hydroculture. It means, as you may have guessed, growing plants in water rather than in soil. Plants do not need earth around them in order to grow – they get moisture and minerals from it, but these can be supplied direct by dosing them with a nutrient solution instead. Anyone who has grown a hyacinth in a glass, or started off an avocado stone by sitting it in a jar of water has had a go at hydroculture.

It does away with two problems on the house-plant front – wrong watering techniques, and soil-borne pests and diseases. It also takes care of holidays since the plants, when grown this way, can go for three weeks without attention. Why, you might ask, if you can grow plants in water alone, do they die if you overwater them? The answer is that they adapt themselves to hydroculture by growing a different root system, so unless you're starting from scratch, with seeds or cuttings, the plants take a week or so to get used to hydroculture, so if you want to have a go, it's best to use a fully-grown plant which can take the shock. And before you switch it to its new container every scrap of soil must be washed off its roots.

Soil has one very important job to do – it supports the plants firmly in the ground. We can't simply grow house plants afloat in bowls of water, they need anchoring. The sturdier ones can be simply poked into a few pebbles stuck in sand, with a little charcoal to keep the water sweet. Otherwise we have to use Vermiculite, gravel or a purpose-made 'inert' substance like clay husks or granules. In fact you can now buy complete hydroculture kits.

Leave a bowl of water to stand for a day or two before you use it for hydroculture, that helps to get rid of the chlorine in it and brings it up to room temperature. Don't ever use artificially softened water for the job. It's a good idea, too, to let the plant have a rest, before it is put in its new home, in a bowl of plain water. When planting time comes, carefully poke a hole in the aggregate with a pencil, and pop it in. You can grow on a cutting quite simply, with its roots in a bottle the hydroculture way, but choose coloured glass, or exclude the light, otherwise an unpleasant green film will line the glass.

Upkeep is simple once you've got under way. You simply dose the plant occasionally with one of the fertilisers which is specially made for the job, following the instructions on the packet.

This is not really a game for beginners, but why not try it with a spare cutting? Or play safe and use one of the ready planted kits.

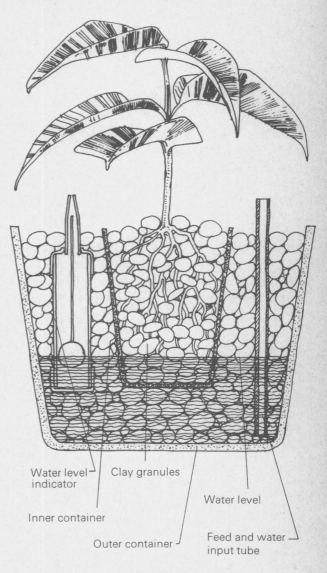

Cross-section of a plant grown in a hydroculture kit

Water level indicator

Clay granules

Inner container

Water level

Outer container

Feed and water input tube

Planting a Bottle Garden

'What's the difference between a bottle garden and a terrarium?' asked Mrs. Q. 'I've got an old fish tank I thought I might plant up. Someone said I should use it like a bottle garden, but I'm not sure . . .'

'There's no real difference between the two,' we told her, 'but it's easier to get at the plants in a terrarium – you will need a lid for yours, of course.'

'Can things really stay alive, shut up like that?' asked Mrs. Q.

'They not only survive, but they thrive,' we told her, 'if you choose the right plants. A bottle garden is self-watering – moisture never escapes but simply condenses and runs back into the soil. First, clean your tank thoroughly, then put a layer of gravel and charcoal on its floor. Cover this with seed compost taking care no soil clings to the sides (if you are using a bottle, shoot the soil in through a funnel), then plant. If it's a bottle garden, use a teaspoon tied to a stick to make holes in the compost, then lower plants down on a piece of wire and firm them in with the spoon. Don't overwater, just moisten with a spray. If it seems too damp and steamy when the top is on, leave it off to allow it to clear.'

'What can I plant?' asked Mrs. Q.

'Anything that likes humidity', we said. 'Calatheas, fittonias and peperomias, African violets too, ivy, *Hedera helix*, goes well, and *Sansevieria hahnii*, *Pilea cadierei* and *Pilea microphylla*. For larger containers try dracaena and the smaller kinds of codiaeum. The spider plant grows well this way, as do wild plants that live in woodland settings. Once you've got your garden going it needs little attention, but if some of the plants get too tall, remove them and replant with other miniatures.'

Hanging Baskets

'Hanging baskets look pretty, but I think they're more trouble than they're worth,' said Mrs. D. 'The one I had last summer kept drying out. I lost all my plants except the geranium.'

'They are difficult to keep going because of watering,' we said, 'but there are things you can do to make them easier to manage. First of all you must plant them up properly, late spring is the best time. Stand the basket in a bucket while you fill it. Line it first with sphagnum moss, if you can get it, then with green or black plastic. Poke plants through at this stage if you are putting trailers underneath. Place broken crocks and charcoal in the centre bottom, then fill up with compost, adding trailing plants through the sides as you go – make sure they're firmed down. Use a potting mixture laced with peat.'

'I don't really know what to put in it, this year,' said Mrs. D. 'I always did geraniums with alyssum and blue trailing lobelias, but I'm rather fed up with that.'

'There's a whole host of plants that can be "hung",' we said. 'Succulents like the Christmas Cactus and trailing sedums are ideal for a basket indoors that is likely to dry out often and has to contend with rising heat; the Spider Plant too. But for your porch you will want more colour: what about petunias and variegated ivy, for instance, trailing fuchsias and nasturtiums? Begonias are good too. For a touch of silver add *Helichrysum angustifolium*, and, for a splash of yellow, some calceolaria.

'There are so many plants for hanging baskets – achimenes, trailing campanulas, nepeta, even sweet peas, and you can also grow herbs in them. There is only one way to water them, and that's by immersing them in a bucket. They will need doing at least once a day in high summer, tiresome, but worth it!'

Repotting

'When do I repot?' is a frequent question we are asked. Plants which are carefully tended and do well will probably want repotting within a year. As they grow they produce so many roots they become potbound and need moving to larger containers. If you suspect your plant is getting too big for its pot, check for a number of signs. *Roots* will start appearing through the drainage holes at the bottom of the pot, *leaves* will start wilting soon after watering because there isn't enough compost to hold the water. New leaves will remain small, while older leaves turn yellow and drop off because the limited nutrients are being concentrated in the growing tip of the plant. Altogether it won't be looking quite as healthy and attractive as it used to.

As a visual check, turn the pot upside down while holding its top in the palm of your hand with the stem between the middle two fingers, and tap the edge of the pot on the table. The

plant with its root ball will ease out of the pot into your hand. Examine the root ball carefully; if it consists of a mass of roots coiling round each other with very little soil showing, then it certainly needs repotting.

Pick a pot only one size up on the last one, or the plant will feel lost. If you are using a new clay pot, soak it for at least 24 hours beforehand as it is very absorbent and will otherwise soak up water from the compost inside.

Because of their confined root space, plants in pots need the best soil. It should be free from pests and diseases, and sterilised before use. That rules out ordinary garden soil. Buy potting composts like John Innes, or the soil-less composts sold under various brand names. Place enough soil into the bottom of the new pot to bring the root ball, when it is put in, up to an inch from the top of the pot. Position the root ball in the centre, and fill in around it with compost until you reach the original soil level. Give the plant a little shake, firm the compost down with your fingers but don't press too hard. Tap the pot on the table to settle the soil, then water. Spray the leaves with water and keep the plant in a cool shady place for a couple of days to let it settle.

When should you repot? Late spring is the best time, and the operation should give the plant enough nutrient in the new soil to last it for six months without feeding. A young, vigorous, fast-growing house plant, however, should be watched, it could well need a fertiliser top-up after three months.

Holiday Care

We were surprised to hear Mrs. T say that she was worried about going on holiday. 'It's my house plants,' she said, 'the last time I left them to be looked after, they all died.'

Well, there probably wouldn't have been any casualties if Mrs. T had given the plant sitter precise instructions on just how much water and feeding each plant should have. But there are a number of things you can do, yourself, without having to depend on others. For a start, for just an absence of a few days, you can put the plant pot in a basin of wet sand. If you plan to be away for a longer spell, first pinch off all the flowers and buds to reduce the amount of water the plant will want. Then take it away from direct sunlight and pack it in a box or basin filled with damp peat or screwed-up wet newspaper.

If one plant is your pride and joy, water it and then put a clear plastic bag over it, holding this away from the leaves with a wire frame. Make a couple of small holes in the bag and seal it round the side of the pot with elastic or sticky tape. In the case of several plants, it's a good idea to put them in the sink and make a plastic tent over them, after watering them.

The bathroom is an ideal place to store plants if there is plenty of light; sit a cluster of pots in about an inch of water in the bath. The average bath plug will allow the water to seep away over the couple of weeks you are not there and the sides of the bath will reflect the light. Or, for more control over the situation, buy some proprietary capillary matting and spread it on the draining board with one end dangling well into a sink full of water. Put your pots on the mat. The capillary action will pull up the water into the compost through the holes in the bottom of the pots. Use plastic pots, pressed well down on the matting. Plants in clay pots need a 'wick' pushed up through the drainage hole to connect the matting with the compost – cut off a piece of the matting for this. Have a happy holiday!

Let's Get Together

Mrs. J was talking to us about the problem of getting a clutch of house plants to do well together. 'I'm always being told that if you put three or four plants into one container they will create their own climate and flourish, but I never get anything like that response.'

'You have got to choose compatible types of plants,' we told her. 'It's no good putting together cacti and a codiaeum, for example. One needs a high temperature and dry air, while although the other needs high temperatures too, a high humidity is required to go with it. Provided the plants are compatible, that is, they like the same temperature, the same amount of water, light and warmth, then

they'll thrive. But, having said that, it's amazing how tolerant apparently unsuitable partners can be, provided the conditions aren't too wet and too cold. They seem in some way to accommodate each other. You can either simply place a selection of plants in pots close together, or buy a special planter to put them all in. Or there is a way between the two that is probably the best solution of all: keep the plants in their individual containers, but plunge them together into one larger outer one. They don't have to stay in pots, you could transfer them into black polythene bags, the kind that commercial growers use. These fit together better in cramped space. And this way you can vary the watering routine a little from plant to plant.'

'Which plants make the best bedfellows?' asked Mrs. J.

'You could make a very showy display of foliage plants mixing dracaenas with codiaeums and begonias,' we told her. 'Tradescantia and the ivies would make good trailers, with *Philodendron scandens* in the background. The Spider Plant makes a friendly neighbour, and if you want a fern, choose a small one like pellaea. African violets like the moist climate of a mixed planting. Dieffenbachias and philodendrons go well together and can be joined by the monstera for a bolder display with, perhaps, colourful caladiums as well.

'The thing you must remember when you do a massed planting of this kind is to keep an eye on the numbers. Plants grown this way grow so well, especially in warm conditions, that they can quickly become overcrowded, and then you will have to weed some out.'

Chink Small!

'If space is at a premium, a garden made out of miniatures makes a marvellous decoration for a tabletop,' we suggested to Mrs. F, who wanted something unusual to give a friend.

'But I'm not very keen on those rather stiff, Japanesy arrangements,' she said. 'With miniature pagodas, mirrors and things.'

'A miniature garden doesn't have to be like that at all,' we told her. 'It's simply because the Japanese are so fond of miniaturising things that so many gardens have that oriental look. You can make a very interesting but formal garden from cacti or other succulents, but there are lots of other things as well – small alpines, for instance, or you can use very small versions of popular plants like begonias, and African violets. The main thing to remember is that everything you plant must "get on" in terms of temperature and water, or you will have great difficulty in keeping it going. Miniature bulbs are another idea for a gift garden. You can buy tiny daffodils that are almost as small as snowdrops.'

'How do I set about making this garden, then?' asked Mrs. F.

'First you have got to find a shallow container, anything too deep gives the game away and looks out of proportion,' we said. 'For a garden out of doors you can't beat a stone sink, but for indoors the best thing to do is to look for a tray of some sort – the dishes used for developing photographic prints are light and easy to obtain. You will need to bore some drainage holes in the container; cover these with broken crocks, than a layer of pebbles, peat, and finally compost. Decorate the surface with miniature "rocks". Now you can look for your plants – tiny versions of ivy, miniscule roses, cushion plants like saxifrage or raoulia, which makes an attractive blue "grass". The rosette-like sempervivums make a good choice for this kind of tiny garden too. You can experiment with miniature trees, or even miniaturise tiny saplings by cutting back their roots. The best way to do this is to plant the sapling in a small cream carton with holes for drainage, and snip the roots off each time they poke through. Remember to water well and often and not to feed the plants or they will grow too big!'

Battered Babies

One of the strangest phone calls we have ever had was from a lady who asked us: 'What can you do with a palm tree that has split in half?'

'How did it happen?' we asked, aghast.

'It was *thrown* across a room,' she replied.

We didn't like to ask any questions after that! Accidents do happen to plants. They get knocked off ledges and tables by pets. Well-meaning children yank them out of their pots, or a wind-blown curtain may catch them. Plants also get polluted by paraffin or gas fumes and overwatering may take its toll.

Broken Plants

If a plant has been broken almost clean through, then there is nothing for it but to cut the affected part off. But don't throw it away, if the break is fairly new you can probably take a cutting from the piece. If the plant is in a generally battered condition, but has several branches on it, check on the cuttings situation (see page 59). It might be best to take several cuttings while you can, and discard the parent.

If the break is more of a bend and the plant has not snapped completely through but is still connected by at least half the thickness of the stem, then on a fully grown plant it's worth-while putting sticky tape round the break. Better still use medical plaster and a splint to bind up the stem in the hope that it will knit together again. If this shows signs of failing, use the top of the stem as a cutting.

Leaf Damage

Burned, holed or diseased leaves should be cut off the plant. Browned tips should be trimmed with scissors and there is no point in keeping yellowed leaves on a plant either, unless you've found the trouble is the acid balance of the soil, when they may recover. Diseased leaves should be burned or thrown away, not left lying at the base of the plant.

Watering – first aid

A plant that has been underwatered should respond to treatment – a good bath – within two or three hours. It's a good idea to spray the leaves too. A plant that has been over-watered can be tackled too, see page 21. If all else fails, try taking cuttings from it.

Give 'Em a Rest!

Miss L was describing the fine display her house plants had made during the past summer. 'Should I give them a jolly good feed now, and plenty of water, after all that work?' she asked us.

'You should only water them like that if they're staying in a warm room,' we said. 'And as for feeding, you're right to realise that they have worked hard. What they probably need now is a rest, just as we do after a strenuous effort. It's their equivalent of a holiday. Although the more tropical house plants don't have seasons in the way our garden plants do, they don't keep going non-stop for twelve months of the year. They all need a dormant period, and they shouldn't be forced into continual growth by being left in too warm a spot. So, when the daylight hours shorten and the temperature drops, put the plants that have finished their season out of direct sunlight, in a slightly cooler, draught-free spot. Before putting them into their winter quarters, tidy them up, pick off any dead flowers or leaves and wipe over those leaves that are still on the plant. Scratch the surface of the soil to aerate it a little. It's important to check out the lowest temperature your particular plants can take – around 10°C (50°F) suits quite a large number of them. If you're stuck with a higher temperature than the plant needs, you'll have to ease it into dormancy with careful watering – only give it moisture at the beginning of the day so that any excess has a chance to evaporate before the temperature drops at night. The cooler the room, the less water you must give – cold, damp soil is a plant killer.

'Cacti and succulents which have been put into a cool conservatory or bedroom with little or no heat can stay without attention until mid-spring. But don't be dominated by the rule book; if the succulents, in particular, are in a rather warm place, a once-a-month drink won't hurt. Geraniums too, should be practically dried off, cold and damp conditions will make their stems rot.

After the winter hibernation, start the new spring with a gentle awakening. Most human beings like a quiet welcome to the day. Plants are just the same. Put each plant pot in a bucket of tepid rainwater and leave it until the air bubbles stop rising from the compost. Leave them to drain and put them in medium light. Watch the leaves, and when there are signs of growth, continue watering regularly. This may well be the time when you want to repot them, or to top them up with fresh compost. Start feeding your plants as soon as they show signs of really growing away, but err on the side of caution, under- rather than overdose them or you may do more harm than good.

Some plants confuse us and reverse the order of things, resting in the summer and growing in the winter. These include acidanthera, azalea, some begonias and some chrysanthemums. African violets often come into this category, so does the Christmas Cactus, the Jerusalem Cherry, camellias, forced bulbs, and two top gift plants – cyclamen and poinsettia. These need different treatment, so check out their requirements when you buy them, see also pages 34 to 45.

Propagation-Simple Multiplication

More plants for our money, that is what we all want, so it's a good idea to use your stock to build up a supply of new plants with which to enlarge your collection, to swop with other house-plant owners, to give away, or even to sell. Some plants, the geranium for example, positively benefit by having cuttings chopped off them for it encourages them to grow bushier.

There's no mystery about the different ways of starting new plants – from seed, by cuttings, division or layering – and anyone can do it. Seeds are the slowest, division is instant, but can only be applied to some things. Each plant has a method that suits it best, so we've listed them for you on this chart. If you've never tried propagating before, or if your only experience is limited to sticking a piece of tradescantia into a jar of water, join us. In the next few pages we'll be giving you the know-how you need.

Get into the habit of *using* the bits you prune off your house plants when you groom them. Grow them on, or save the seed from flowers and have a go at growing a new crop. After all, it is free!

Save Your Own Seed

Almost anything that flowers can be propagated from seed if you have the patience to wait. Pick off the seed pods the moment they are beginning to dry and shrivel on the plant. Put them somewhere warm and dry for a month and they are ready to use.

A Hundred House plants – and the Best Way to Propagate Them

Abutilon	stem cuttings, seed
Achimenes	stem cuttings, leaf cuttings, seed
Aechmea	offsets
African Violet (Saintpaulia)	division, leaf cuttings, seed
Aglaonema (Chinese Evergreen)	division, offsets
Aloe	offsets
Anthurium	offsets, seed, division
Aphelandra	stem cuttings
Araucaria	seed, cuttings
Asparagus Fern	division
Aspidistra	division
Aucuba (laurel)	stem cuttings
Azalea	layering, stem cuttings
Baby's Tears (*Helxine soleirolii*)	stem cuttings
Begonia	stem cuttings, leaf cuttings
Bird's Nest Fern	spores
Bromeliads	offsets
Bulbs	offsets
Cacti	stem cuttings, offsets
Caladium	division of tubers
Calathea	division
Callistemon	stem cuttings
Camellia	stem cuttings, leaf bud cuttings

Chamaedorea (Palm)	division	Hibiscus	stem cuttings
Chenille Plant (*Acalypha hispida*)	stem cuttings	Hippeastrum	offsets
		Hoffmannia	stem cuttings
Chlorophytum	layering	Hoya	stem cuttings
Christmas Cactus	stem cuttings	Hydrangea	stem cuttings
Chrysanthemum	stem cuttings	Impatiens	stem cuttings
Cissus	stem cuttings	Ipomoea	stem cuttings (*I. tricolor* by seed)
Citrus	stem cuttings, pips		
Codiaeum (Croton)	stem cuttings	Jasminum	stem cuttings
Coleus	stem cuttings, seed	Kalanchoe	leaf cuttings
Cordyline	stem cuttings, root cuttings	Lapageria	seed
		Maranta	division
Crassula	stem cuttings, leaf cuttings	Mimosa	stem cuttings, seed
		Monstera (Swiss Cheese Plant)	layering, stem cuttings
Crown of Thorns	stem cuttings		
Cryptanthus	offsets	Myrtus (Myrtle)	stem cuttings
Cyclamen	seed	Nertera	division
Cyperus	division	Pachystachys	stem cuttings
Datura	stem cuttings	Passiflora	seed, stem cuttings
Dieffenbachia	division, stem sections	Pelargonium (Geranium)	stem cuttings
Dracaena	stem cuttings, root cuttings	Peperomia	stem cuttings, leaf cuttings
Echeveria	stem cuttings, leaf cuttings	Persea (Avocado)	from stones
		Philodendron	stem cuttings
Eranthemum	stem cuttings	Pilea	stem cuttings
Erica	stem cuttings	Piper	stem cuttings
Eucalyptus	seed	Platycerium	offsets
Euphorbia	stem cuttings	Plumbago	stem cuttings, seed
Fatshedera	stem cuttings	Rhoicissus	stem cuttings
Fatsia	stem cuttings, seed	Sansevieria	leaf cuttings, division
Ferns	spores, in some cases division	Schefflera	seed
		Sedums	leaf cuttings
Ficus	stem cuttings, air layering	Sempervivums	by plantlets
		Senecio (Cinerarias)	seed
Fittonia	stem cuttings	Solanum (Jerusalem	seed
Freesia	seed, corms	Stephanotis	stem cuttings
Fuchsia	stem cuttings	Strelitzia	division, seed
Gardenia	stem cuttings	Thunbergia	stem cuttings, seed
Gloxinia	stem cuttings, seed, tubers	Tolmiea	plantlets
		Tradescantia	stem cuttings
Grevillea	seed	Veltheimia	offsets
Gynura	stem cuttings	Vriesea	offsets
Haworthia	offsets	Yucca	root cuttings, offsets
Hedera (Ivy)	stem cuttings	Zebrina	stem cuttings

Seeds and Seedling Trouble

'I bought a propagator from a chain store to raise some plants to give away as Christmas presents, but suddenly all the seedlings have collapsed inside it!' Miss J had hit upon the idea of growing house plants from seed, so naturally she was disappointed when they flagged and then died off.

'Did you give them plenty of light?' we asked.

'I don't think I did at first,' she told us. 'When they came up they were long and thin and all bent towards the window, so I turned the box round and they straightened up. They had plenty of water, too.'

'Well, then that's not likely to be the cause,' we said. 'Lack of light can kill tender young seedlings off very quickly. Some people start seeds off in the dark, and don't bring them out into the light soon enough, or they switch them from darkness to bright sun in one go – it's best to put them in the shade first. Ideally seeds should be started off with heat from below. This encourages them to make good roots before the shoots grow too tall to be serviced properly. Tell us, did the seedlings go thin and brown at soil level before they collapsed? If they did, then "damping-off" is your problem. This is a fungus disease and you must be ultra-careful and sterilise the box in which you start them off; use sterile compost too, like John Innes seed compost. It's also a good idea to use a fungicide.'

'It sounds very complicated,' said Miss J.

'Well you are, after all, trying to grow your own tropical plants,' we said. 'Here's how you do the sowing. Press the moistened compost down gently, and then spread the seed on top – sowing it thinly because overcrowding encourages damping off. Sprinkle a thin layer of soil over the seeds and firm the surface down again.

Then you cover the seeds with a sheet of polythene, glass, or the propagator lid and take a look at them every two or three days. They will probably need a little water but don't knock them sideways with it, stand the container in water and let it seep in from underneath.'

Cuttings

'Some people seem to be able to pull a piece of twig off a bush and grow a tree from it, but any cuttings I've tried to root have never taken.'

This was a common complaint we had from house-plant owners. Yet, because the temperature can be controlled more accurately indoors, you should be able to take cuttings very easily. But a lot of people seem to be trying to grow the wrong bits! Another thing that often goes wrong is that the piece of plant is left to lie around after it has been lopped off while the owner searches for a pot and some compost. With most plants speed is of the essence, and if the cut edge dries out you may not be successful.

There are exceptions to this rule, and these are the plants whose stems contain a kind of rubbery substance. The Rubber Plant is one, geraniums have a different kind of sap, and so do cacti. In these cases it's better to leave the cuttings for a while because then their ends get sealed up by their own sap, and are less likely to be attacked by fungi. Most house-plant cuttings are known as softwood ones as the stems are pliable and not woody. When taking cuttings the idea is to remove a growing shoot and put it into compost so that it will grow a set of roots. The ideal material for this is a strong teenage shoot, nothing too young and tender, nothing too old and tough; a thick healthy piece. Cut off a shoot at least 10 cm (4 in) long, more if the plant is big. The cutting should have at least three joints in its stem, places where the leaves spring from. Take off some of the bottom leaves as this part of the stem will be going into the soil, but leave two or three leaves on top, no more, for the plant will have a struggle at first while growing roots to maintain water supplies to more than that. Remove any flower buds for the same reason.

Have your container ready, cut a small slice off the bottom of the cutting and dip the end in the hormone rooting compound intended for softwood cuttings, if you have one. Now insert it firmly into the rooting compost. What kind should this be? A light soil is essential: a mix of peat and Vermiculite, for instance, with a little sand, will suit them fine.

Layering
...on the ground

'My Spider Plant hasn't had any babies!' This was a complaint we got again and again from disgruntled owners. And the reason in most cases, we found, was that the plant simply wasn't old enough to start a family – only mature chlorophytums produce plantlets from the ends of the thin runners. Sometimes, though, a Spider Plant will delay producing babies if it is living in cramped conditions. This is a plant that loves hanging baskets – it seems to be able to spread itself in them. So if you're having trouble, try potting your plant up in one.

Chlorophytum plantlets are among the easiest things to grow on. We do it by layering, as it is called, and we use the same technique for several other house plants who reproduce in this way, *Saxifraga sarmentosa*, for instance, which isn't called Mother of Thousands for nothing, and *Tolmiea menziesii*, the Pick-a-back Plant. The plantlets of all these will root quite happily and easily once they come in contact with soil, in the meantime living by the equivalent of an umbilical cord from the mother plant. The easiest way to root new plants is to cut them off the run-ner, leaving about 1 cm (½ in) of it still attached, and plant them into a potting compost making sure the tiny crowns are not covered. But if you do this, the shock of being severed from the mother plant means the baby takes time to recover and grows slowly at first.

A better way is to surround the mother plant with a ring of satellite pots and peg the plantlets down into these using a hairpin. Be careful not to stretch the runners or the plantlets will tend to lift clear of the soil. When they have rooted and are growing well, you can cut the cord.

Some ferns produce runners, and it seems a waste not to propagate them in this way. But if your home is dry you may not have noticed the runners at all, for if there is not enough humidity they shrivel up before producing tiny ferns on the end. The answer to this is to choose a fern and grow it temporarily in a terrarium or a make-shift humid house made from a tent of clear plastic. With patience you'll find runners will appear, and they can be pegged down into pots in the usual way. Once they're going well mother and baby can come out of incubation.

Layering

...in the air

'My Rubber Plant has gone tall and straggly, it's got hardly any leaves on it'. This was another regular query we had, a point made about avocado plants as well. A plant that has gone this way, and which refuses to respond to the old trick of pinching out the growing point to make it bush, is a good candidate for air layering. The technique sounds drastic but usually works like a dream.

Choose the best shoot for the job (if you're dealing with a one-stemmed item you have no choice, anyway) and make an upward cut in the stem with a sharp knife at a point below the tip where you'd like the roots of your new plant to be. The cut should be about 2.5 to 4 cm (1 to 1½ in) long, and should bite into the stem by about one-third. There's no reason why you shouldn't lay the plant on its side to do this. Push a sliver of wood – a matchstick is fine – into the cut to keep it open,

and dust the cut well with hormone rooting powder. Now make a parcel around the area by wrapping it up in moist sphagnum moss and tying this firmly in place. What you are doing is making sure that the top end of the plant, the piece you want to grow on, is still getting its water and nourishment from the roots but that any food the leaves produce stays up top where it is needed. Enclose the sphagnum moss in a further wrapper, this time made from clear polythene which acts as a window so you can see what is going on. Secure the plastic around the stem with insulating tape or plant ties, making sure it keeps the moisture in.

After six to eight weeks when a good growth of roots should be poking through the moss, take off the bandage, cut right through the stem just below your original incision, and grow on your new plant.

Simple Division

Two plants for the price of one, sometimes more than two – that's what you get from root division, and fortunately a lot of house plants can be propagated this way.

It's a simple method of cutting or pulling the plant, roots and all, into two, sometimes more, pieces, and replanting them again in separate pots. Most plants which can be treated in this way need to be divided from time to time otherwise they will overcrowd their pot, their growth slows right down and the centre of the plant may even die off.

'I'm told you can propagate African violets by splitting them in half,' said Mrs. U, 'but I'm frightened I shall kill mine, how do you do it?'

'You can quite easily increase your stock of African violets that way,' we told her. 'You can do the same sort of thing with lots of other house plants too, maybe you have some in your home . . . many ferns with crowns can be split, so can palms, primulas, and many of the alpines – almost anything that is clumpy. Mother-in-law's Tongue (sansevieria is another and so is maranta.'

'How do I set about it? I'm terrified,' said Mrs. U.

'Well, first take a good look at the plant, have a feel around its base and locate how many different little "clumps" there are to it. Each piece must have its own set of roots.'

'I think I'll only try splitting it in half, not more,' said Mrs. U.

'Well, divide it roughly in half with your fingers,' we said, 'and part the foliage. Make quite sure that each part has plenty of root attached, then slice or pull the plant apart down the centre, using your fingers or a sharp knife. Lift the plant from the pot, disentangle it, then place one piece in a new pot – make sure you have it ready – and put the other one back in the centre of its original container.'

'Is that all?' Mrs. U sounded relieved.

'Yes,' we told her. 'There is another kind of division that is even simpler if you have a plant growing from a rhizome – those thick, fleshy underground stems. In this case just cut off a section with a sprouting piece on it and re-bury it in another pot, placing it as far down in the soil as it was before.'

'I'll certainly have a go with the African Violet,' said Mrs. U.

'When you've mastered that, we'll show you how to take leaf cuttings from it as well,' we promised. 'Don't forget too that bulbs often grow tiny bulblets – and the same goes for corms. These can be taken off and replanted. They take several years to form flowers but are well worth keeping. And a tuberous begonia can be increased by breaking off any side pieces which have little shoots on them.'

New Plants From Leaves (Leaf Cuttings)

'Is it really true that you can stick a piece of leaf into the ground and it will grow, just like that?' Mr. K rang us to query this because he'd broken a leaf off a plant in his office and his secretary had told him he could grow it on.

'It depends what the plant is,' we told him, 'some of them, especially the sansevieria, will sprout new shoots and roots from just a small section of leaf.'

'How amazing,' Mr. K was impressed. 'This is one of those begonias with big decorative leaves.'

'In that case,' we told him, 'you take leaf cuttings through the veins. Choose a healthy leaf, cut a 5 cm (2 in) triangle out of it with the prominent main vein running through the middle and ending at the point. Have some potting compost ready, and push the cutting, point first, into the pot. Cover with glass or clear plastic and leave it for a week or so, and it should form roots.'

'I've never heard anything so incredible,' said Mr. K. 'I suppose it isn't *really* complicated to do.'

'It sounds more difficult than it is,' we told him. 'But the easiest leaf cuttings of all are done from long, stiff-leaved plants like the famous Mother-in-law's Tongue, where you simply chop off a piece with a knife and poke it into some compost – and it works well with lots of succulents. Another kind of leaf cutting is the one you do with the African Violet – simply cut off the leaf, stalk and all, where it joins the stem or comes out of the base, and insert the end of the stalk into some potting compost.'

'What else can be grown on from leaves?' asked Mr. K.

'Well, gloxinias for a start,' we said, 'and cyperus. With the Rubber Plant, you can take a leaf bud cutting – that's really worth doing because the plants are so expensive, but you have to sacrifice a side branch to do it. Cut the leaves off that stem with a sharp knife or razor, taking off with them a sliver of the stem itself with some of the inner tissues attached. Inside this, hopefully, is a leaf bud which should produce a new plant. Put your leaf cutting into some good potting compost and firm it in, it will probably be at a slanting angle to the soil but that doesn't matter. Soon a new plant should start to grow.'

Bringing Up Baby

There's the same feeling of pride about bringing a new plant into the home as proud parents get when they bring a new baby back from hospital. And if you've grown it yourself from a cutting or from seed, then it's even more special. But, as with a child, it takes time to find out just how to handle a young plant.

Like babies, fledgling plants need several basic things to be happy: warmth, food and drink and an environment that suits it. So bring it up the right way from the start and it will reward you by flourishing.

Warmth

Do make sure the temperature is right, and if you're not quite sure err on the cool side. A plant that is kept in a room a little too cold for it will simply make rather slow growth, no more harm can come to it than that. But a plant that is struggling with too-hot conditions is not likely to survive for long, it simply hasn't got the stamina to cope at this stage. A baby plant will show you quickly that the temperature's too hot by wilting, because it simply doesn't have the root system to send up more moisture speedily to the leaves as they need it.

In fact, some of our best-known house plants prefer cool rooms, especially at baby stage – the Spider Plant (chlorophytum) for instance, Mother of Thousands (*Saxifraga sarmentosa*,) and the Wandering Sailor (tradescantia). Beware a temperature that goes up and down like a yo-yo, fluctuating heat and cold will cause a chill, so will draughts. If you have a real see-saw temperature problem, then only the chlorophytum and the aspidistra plus, possibly, the ivies (hedera) can cope.

Food

Young plants need a cocktail of chemicals to keep them going and growing, not just the Big Three – nitrogen, potassium and phosphorus – but magnesium, calcium and iron, plus traces of other minerals. And the easiest way to dose them with the right balance is to buy a proprietary plant food. If you choose one that is fed into the soil, be careful, when you water the plant, that none of the mix touches the young leaves, or it may well burn them. A more up-to-date way of coping is to use a foliar feed. This is sprayed on the leaves in a fine mist, and works more quickly. Either way, a growing plant will want feeding once a fortnight but always follow the instructions carefully, never make the mix too strong or it may kill the plant off. The moment growth seems to have stopped and its rest season has arrived, or if it looks at all sickly, stop feeding the plant for the time being – like any invalid, it needs a rest before it steps up its appetite again.

Drink

The right watering is vital for a baby plant. It must have enough to keep it going, but it simply hasn't the strength to stand up to an owner who is over-enthusiastic with a watering can. Tender young roots rot, often the stems become prey to fungus diseases like botrytis or, in the case of geraniums, blackened rotting stems. Lesson number one, then: be sure to put adequate drainage crocks in the pot to start with, and find out what your baby's drinking habits are. If you have a bad track record of overwatering, then spread a few hints around . . maybe someone will buy you a meter which shows you whether the soil needs watering or not, or switch to Hydroculture instead (see page 47).

A Happy Home

If your baby was shop-bought, then the pot in which you bring it home is not likely to be one in which it should stay. Plants for sale are often put in very temporary containers. There are all kinds of pots for plants – ceramic, styrofoam, plastic or clay – but you're most likely to be faced with a choice of the latter two. Which is best? Maybe we're old-fashioned but we like clay pots best of all. They absorb moisture and 'breathe' out moisture through their sides, and the same goes for air. They have two disadvantages: they do tend to dry out quicker, and they break. Plastic pots come in a wider range of colours,

they're lighter to handle, usually cheaper, and plants in them need watering less often, so if you're a weekend-away person, or garden in an office, then a plastic pot may be the best choice. But watch your watering because they can be swamped much more easily, and its more difficult to put right.

Baby plants that are making good headway will want repotting often, so keep an eye on their roots. Don't be tempted to put a small plant in a big pot to save work, it makes it feel insecure and it won't make much headway. The only exception is the monstera (see page 44). Soil and sunshine are two other important items: *do* use a correct mix (see page 46) and *don't* put your plant on the window-sill in strong sun, it's tender young leaves just can't take it.

Plants for Particular Places

Put a house plant in the right situation and see how it thrives. It's amazing how fast it can grow given the right conditions, the right temperature too. But how often does this happen? Not as frequently as one would like, yet very often it's only a matter of shifting the plants around, putting direct light haters away from the window, bring those who want to soak up the sunshine to the forefront instead. Here's our guide line to help you decide where you should put what, and what you should grow.

Plants for a sunny situation, warm room

Ananas	*Euphorbia milii*
Beloperone	Hibiscus
Ceropegia	*Pandanus veitchii*
Clerodendrum	*Ruellia macrantha*
Clianthus	Tradescantia
Codiaeum	Zebrina
Coleus	

Plants for a shady situation, warm room

Achimenes	Gloxinia
Adiantum	Maranta
Aglaonema	Monstera
Anthurium	Pachystachys
Aphelandra	Peperomia
Columnea	Philodendron
Cyperus	Saintpaulia
Ficus	Spathiphyllum
Fittonia	*Syngonium podophyllum*

Rooms cool in winter, plenty of light

Abutilon	Hydrangea
Aloe	Kalanchoe
Ampelopsis	Pachyphytum
Bougainvillea	Passiflora
Chlorophytum	Pelargonium
Citrus	Pilea
Cyclamen	Plectranthus
Cytisus	Plumbago
Echeveria	Saxifrage
Erica	Sedum
Grevillea	Solanum
Hebe	Tolmiea

Rooms cool in winter, indirect or bad light

Aspidistra	Howeia
Azalea	Jasminum
Cineraria	*Nertera depressa*
Cissus antarctica	Polystichum
Fatshedera	Rhoicissus
Fatsia	Skimmia
Hedera	*Sparmannia africana*

Plants with spectacular foliage

Adiantum	Fittonia
Aglaonema	*Gynura aurantiaca*
Aloe variegata	Maranta
Asplenium nidus	Monstera
Begonia rex	*Nolina recurvata*
Caladium bicolor	Pellionia

Calathea makoyana
Chamaedorea
  elegans
Codiaeum
Coleus
Dieffenbachia
Dizygotheca
Dracaena
Ficus lyrata

Peperomia
Pilea
Piper crocatum
Platycerium
Sansevieria
Scindapsus aureus
Setcreasea purpurea
Sonerila
  margaritacea

Climbers, trailers for indoor use

Ceropegia
Cissus antarctica
Dioscorea discolor
Ficus pumila
Gynura
Hedera
Helxine soleirolii
Hoya carnosa
Passiflora

Pellionia
Peperomia scandens
Philodendron
Pilea muscosa
Piper
Rhoicissus
Scindapsus
Senecio
  macroglossus
Tradescantia

Plants with scented flowers or leaves

Daphne
Datura
Eucalyptus
Gardenia

Rose Geranium
Jasminum
Lemon-scented
  Verbena

Plants for warm, humid places, like bathrooms

Adiantum
Aphelandra
Caladium
Calathea
Codiaeum

Dieffenbachia
Dracaena
Grevillea robusta
Saintpaulia
Scindapsus aureus

Plants for ground cover, in group plantings

Ficus pumila
Fittonia
Gynura

Hedera helix
Helxine soleirolii
Selaginella
  kraussiana

Plants for fun

Avocado (grow your own from a stone)
Citrus mitis (make your own marmalade from its tiny bitter oranges)
Coffea arabica (grow your own coffee!)
Cocos weddelliana (Dwarf Coconut Palm)
Desmodium gyrans (the Telegraph Plant, its leaves perform semaphore moves in sunlight)
Ginger (plant a piece of green root)
Maranta leuconeura kerchoveana (Prayer Plant, it folds its leaves like hands in prayer as night falls)
Mimosa pudica (the Sensitive Plant, its leaves fold if you touch them)

Succulents for the easy life

Aloes
Echeverias
Euphorbias

Haworthias
Kalanchoes
Sedums

To show succulents off to the best advantage, take time to choose the right container. They do look rather dull in straightforward flower-pots, but take on a new look altogether in something more exciting.

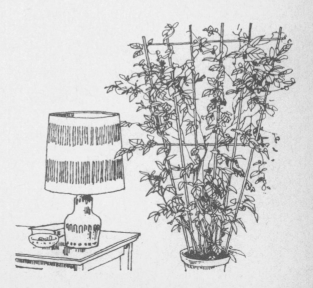

Don't Be Afraid of the Dark!

The average house, alas, is nowhere near as light and bright as a conservatory, in fact the rooms are surprisingly dingy. One way to find out the level of light is to take a light meter, the kind photographers use, and see what it registers as you walk around. Halls are notoriously dim places, yet just the spot where you might want to put some plants. The furthest corner from the window is another obviously dim spot. 'Service' rooms too, like kitchens and bathrooms, have a disppointing amount of light.

This point came home to Mr. X who wanted to buy a flat-warming present for his daughter in the form of a plant. 'What can you suggest?'

Growing case for African violets

he asked us. 'She's sharing a flat in the City with some friends from her office, but the trouble is that it's a dark place, all high narrow windows and the sun only seems to shine in a few hours each day because of the tall buildings opposite.'

'It's quite surprising how well some plants will do in dim surroundings,' we told him, 'and of course if you're prepared to use artificial light, you can really go to town. We've heard of African violets thriving in a basement flat where there was no natural light at all. It was all done by strip lighting. When you come to use the natural light available, then it's still surprising how many of the popular foliage plants can be used. After all, many of them grow naturally in jungle shade and the sunlight only reaches them through layers of foliage. Bad lighting rules out most of the flowering plants but not all. Mind you, you can always lessen the gloom in a room from the plant's point of view by using mirrors – place a plant in front of one and it is likely to get twice the amount of light. A table lamp helps too. Switched on close to a plant at the end of the day, it gives the benefit of longer light and the plant will grow larger and better. But one must be careful not to place it too near otherwise the leaves could get scorched. Cold, sunless rooms cause all sorts of other problems: for instance, if conditions are like that, a plant will need less water because the moisture is not being taken in so quickly. If it is watered too much the damp soil will become cold, and this combined with a low room temperature will almost certainly kill the plant.

Mirrors help to lessen the gloom

'Having said that, there are plants which will cope quite happily with dark and rather gloomy conditions. Philodendrons and marantas, for example, prefer shade and should be kept in it for their own health's sake. The good-tempered Rubber Plant too will stand a certain amount, so will the monstera. It's worth remembering that with a little guile you can furnish a dark room with plants as long as you give them only a short spell there at a time, then move them somewhere brighter for a while. And remember, the less light they have the less water they need. A useful rule of thumb to remember, if you are looking for a house plant for a dark place, is that the darker and thicker the leaves are the more they can stand gloom.'

Plants for darkish places

Aglaonema	Monstera
Asparagus	Nephrolepis
Aspidistra	Palms
Ferns	Philodendron
Ficus	Rhoicissus
Maranta	Sansevieria

Plants that need shade

Araucaria	Green Ivies
Begonia	Pellaea
Calathea	Peperomia
Cissus	Platycerium
Dieffenbachia	Syngonium
Fittonia	Vriesea

Some Like It Hot

'What kind of plants can live alongside central heating?' That's a question we're asked time and time again. One good thing about these frequent requests is that by now almost everyone seems to know that the dry, hot atmosphere you get in a centrally heated house or flat is *not*, as you might first think, ideal for bringing up house plants. Basically all plants like the same kind of conditions to live in as people. They don't want to be over hot, or over cold or crowded. And they, too, simply hate draughts. One reason why so many indoor plants die off is that while many of them are used to heat it must be humid as well. Anyone who has been to the Caribbean or the Far East where many of these plants come from, will testify that as you step out of the 'plane it is almost like getting into a sauna bath, the humidity is so high. But not all so-called tropical plants are actually used to heat, so it's wrong to assume they'll love your central heating as much as you do. Some of them come from rain-forest conditions high up in mountains, where the sun doesn't really penetrate that much and it can be quite cool.

Draughts Can Kill!

You might think air conditioning would help plants in a hot atmosphere but quite often it has the reverse effect, for it can cause piercing draughts and there's nothing more calculated to make a plant collapse. The kind of plants with large soft leaves which can stand central heating under normal conditions – and by this we're talking about geraniums, flowering poinsettias and cinerarias – positively hate draughts and very quickly show it by yellowing, drooping and dropping foliage. Even toughies like the aspidistra and sansevieria are harmed by draughts in these conditions,

although they don't always show it immediately. So be careful not to place your plants in the danger zone, particularly in a heated house, such as in a direct line between a door and the windows, or near air-conditioning ducts. Another unexpected source of draughts is a disused fireplace.

Humidity Counts

When the heating is on, we are drawing in cold outside air and raising its temperature by degrees. In doing this we lower its relative humidity by as much as a half. That's why it's so difficult to grow plants indoors out of season, having been happy all summer in natural heat, they sulk, droop and drop their leaves when the heating is switched on and the humidity level goes down.

Watch Your Watering

Centrally heated plants need more watering for the higher the temperature, the drier the air, and the more liquid they must take in to compensate. An occasional spray helps most plants unless they are the hairy-leaved African Violet or the Gloxinia. Palms and bromeliads, in particular, really enjoy frequent misting with water in hot conditions.

Stop that Temperature See-Saw

Although heating may appear, at first, to give plants a nice stable temperature to live in, it's normally switched off at night. Worse than that, many people leave plants on their window-sills in winter, so they bake by day and freeze by night as the window panes almost frost over inside and the plants are trapped between the curtains and the glass.

How to Survive Central Heating

The unhappiest plant of all is usually the one that is put on a window-sill right on top of a radiator, deprived of the moisture it needs, alternately freezing and frying. What can be done? First move it away from the radiator, out of reach of draughts. Next, put a humidifier near it to keep the air moist – no need to buy something expensive, just a bowl of pebbles kept topped up with water will help. Better still plunge each plant pot in a bowl of damp peat and keep it well watered.

Another way to increase humidity is by group therapy: put the plants together if they're growing in heated conditions, and you'll find that as their leaves give off moisture they create a higher level of humidity among themselves. They make much more decorative impact that way, too. Try a temporary arrangement and you'll be surprised at the almost instant difference in their looks. Plants grown in hot dry rooms – and this goes for summer conditions too – should be sprayed regularly with a water mister, and have their leaves groomed. Dust seems to collect on them more frequently than in cold damp conditions, and this dust stops their leaves from 'breathing' as they need to do for proper health and growth.

There's one more problem you may come across on the heating front: air pollution, though it is less of a bogey than it used to be. Natural gas does not kill plants but coal gas can – leaves go patchy yellow or sometimes bleached. Paraffin fumes cause leaves to go brown but if the fumes are that bad, they're probably troubling you, too. Outside pollution can be a problem if you live in, or near an industrial zone. The only way to find out which house plant will stand up to the particular kind of poison that your locality brings is to ask the neighbours about their experiences and proceed by trial and error.

Ways Around the Problem

If you find the fuss and bother of providing special humidity too much to cope with, then there are two other courses open to you – you can switch specifically to desert plants like cacti, or their near relations, the succulents. Succulents, in particular, come in some very colourful versions, and a surprisingly large number of cacti bear flowers (see page 39). Or you can put your plants into the snug safety of a bottle garden or a terrarium (more about those on page 48) where they will certainly thrive. Remember in this case that temperatures can really soar inside glass domes and cases if they are left in full sunlight, so keep them in the shade.

Central Heating

The Survivors – Plants that can cope

Araucaria excelsa	Hedera (Ivy)
Aspidistra	Helxine
Chlorophytum	Hen and Chickens
(Spider Plant)	(*Asplenium*
Christmas Cactus	*bulbiferum*)
Coleus	*Hoya carnosa*
Crown of Thorns	*Neanthe bella*
(*Euphorbia milii*)	Palms
Dracaena marginata	Pelargoniums
Fatshedera	(Geraniums)
Ficus lyrata	Peperomia
(Fiddle-leaf Fig)	Poinsettia
Ficus benjamina	(when in flower)
(Weeping Fig)	Sansevieria
Haworthia	Tradescantia

Office Plants

The office plant is all things to all people. To some of us it's a piece of greenery, lovingly cherished, patted and petted, and well looked after. But to someone else in the same room it may be an ash-tray, a trash-can, a useful place to stub out cigarettes, empty the dregs of a coffee cup. So, one thing all office or factory plants must be is tough and adaptable. They must also, in the main, be window-sill plants as well, as that's the usual spot where they will sit. And, since they're almost certain to have air conditioning and/or central heating to stand up to, they'll probably be prey to the insects which pounce on them in these sort of conditions.

Another item that the office plant has to contend with is a terrific temperature see-saw, especially in winter. Most offices and factories wind down the heating on Friday night, start it up again on Monday – we all know how cold it can be when we first come in on Mondays. The building has been left chill and cold all weekend – and so have the plants. We've met one devoted office gardener who takes her plant home with her at weekends, just because of this very thing. Then there's the time you go on holiday and your colleagues promise they'll look after your plant for you. But it's obvious when you come back, by the browned fallen leaves lying on the soil beneath, that the poor thing has been neglected until a few days before your return.

So, all in all, living in an office or factory is something of an assault course for the average plant. What can be done about it? First, choose the right breed for the job. Second, buy a stout, healthy well-bred specimen – the office is no place to run a nursery.

Group plants together. Whether it's several one-plant owners in a co-operative, or your own collection, a cluster of plants will thrive far better than one on its own. It's a question of humidity of course. But be warned that any pest or disease, like the dreaded red spider mite, will run rampant through the lot if it gets a hold. So watch their health carefully, and have an insecticide spray on hand.

Keep them clean. Office plants are especially prone not just to pollution but to dirt and dust and grit. In fact when you see what you wipe off their leaves in an average week, you wonder what it does to your lungs! Wipe or wash the leaves down regularly with water to which a tiny amount of soap has been added, then rinse. You'll probably need the help of soap to get the grease and dust away. Then use a leaf-shiner, if you like, to perk up the larger leathery-leaved plants, but *not* soft-leaved ones.

Don't forget to feed them. In this, probably the worst environment of all, plants will perk up if they're given a fertiliser feed from time to time; you can buy it in tablet form from your chain store to put into the soil. A foliar feed will help too. Check first though when your plant should be fed. Most of them should be left alone during their rest months, i.e. when they are showing little or no signs of growth and no flowers. But there are some which need the opposite treatment.

Let them have a happy weekend too. Make sure they've had a good drink of water before you go off on Friday. It's a good idea, too, to bring them in off the window-sill in case they get scorched by hot sun, or frozen at night. Being kept in dimmer conditions for a couple of days will stop them transpiring quite so fast and using up their stock of water.

Give them a holiday, sometimes. If you're a keen house-plant collector, switch your possessions around. Bring the office plants home for a spell, replace them with something from stock. But remember too great a change of climate could shock them, so only do it if conditions are right.

They need the best possible soil. Remember they're struggling against difficult conditions and need all the help they can get. Make sure they're well stocked with minerals and other trace elements which will give them healthy growth.

Think in terms of something different. A small bottle garden or terrarium is a fool-proof way to grow plants in office conditions because it creates a humidity all its own. But never stand them on the window-sill for the heat would be too much. Don't forget, too, that there are alternative ways to grow plants: without soil, for instance which gets round the watering problems (see page 47). And if you've space, you can have a near-automatic watering system using capillary matting (see page 51). Think in terms, too, of a miniature garden which doesn't obstruct the view and looks pretty on a window-sill. Or a cluster of cacti – architectural shapes like theirs go well in office surroundings. Then there are some of the stranger succulents, like living stones, the lithops. You could even have a water-garden if you wanted to, there are miniature water-lilies (look for the word *pygmaea* on the end of their names) which can be grown in just 15 to 23 cm (6 to 9 in) of water, as much depth as you get in the average pudding basin!

The Tough Mob

Cacti and other succulents
Chlorophytum (Spider Plant)
Cyperus alternifolius (Umbrella Grass)
Hedera (Ivy)
Nidularium (Bromeliad)
Sansevieria (Mother-in-law's Tongue)
Tradescantia (Wandering Sailor)
Zebrina pendula (Wandering Jew)

The Second Eleven – these can tolerate some shade

Aspidistra
Cissus antarctica (Kangaroo Vine)
Dracaenas
Fatshedera lizei (climber)
Fatsia japonica (False Castor Oil Plant)
Ficus elastica (Rubber Plant)
Monstera (Swiss Cheese Plant)
Philodendron scandens (climber)
Platycerium (Stag's-horn Fern)
Rhoicissus rhomboidea (Grape Ivy – a climber)
Vriesea splendens (Bromeliad)

Kitchen Company

In many ways the kitchen makes an ideal place to grow plants. For, as long as the ventilation is right, they love the slightly humid atmosphere they're likely to get. So if you have a window-sill in your kitchen, clear away those bottles of detergent, the bits and pieces that tend to collect there, and grow some greenery instead. Go one stage further: grow something to eat. Herbs, in particular, make marvellous kitchen companions. You're much more likely to use them in your food if you have them right to hand. Some herbs, chives, for example, are perfectly happy in relatively small pots. But you'll find your mini-herb garden much more rewarding, particularly if you want to use it on a cut-and-come-again basis, if you can group the herbs together in a larger container. A plastic pre-formed window-box, the kind you can buy quite cheaply at garden centres, is ideal for placing on the window-sill inside.

Another item people tend to forget is the hanging basket, which can equally well be hung indoors as out – have it on a pulley over the sink and watering is no longer a problem. Herbs grow well in hanging baskets, but don't just stick them in the top, trail some of the more prostrate ones, like thyme, through the sides. Another interesting way to grow herbs in the kitchen is in spice jars, or better still preserving jars of the wide-necked kind, so you can get your fingers in easily to pick the leaves. Plant and use the jars just like a bottle garden (see page 48) but keep the humidity level down.

Even if you haven't room for herbs in the kitchen on a regular basis, it pays to dig up a few roots of mint, and other favourites like tarragon and marjoram in the autumn and bring them indoors in the warm to grow on while the rest of the plants die down in the garden. Tomato plants make good kitchen company if you train them around the edges of a window like vines. You can take cuttings from them, too, in July, and grow on tomato plants into the winter: just grow on one or two side shoots, as you nip them off in the usual way, then plant them when they have sprouted whiskery roots.

If you're looking for something neat and tidy to liven up the kitchen, then cacti make good companions since they don't have branches or fronds to get in the way on a working top. You can make a whole kitchen collection of greenery too, by growing on scraps – pips and stones and tops of root vegetables. Carrot tops stuck in a saucer of water develop gorgeous feathery foliage rather like a fern. Try parsnip, turnip and beet in the same way. Orange and lemon pips can be coaxed into attractive little bushes or trees. Start them off on top of the boiler, in a pot on a tray – they need plenty of bottom heat. Enclose the pot in a clear plastic bag until you see the first sign of a shoot. The avocado, too, is an attractive addition to the kitchen, and you can even try growing a plant from a coffee bean, provided it hasn't been roasted!

A salad on your window-sill? Why not, if you've got the space. Lettuces thrive this way, endive can be pot-grown so can cucumbers and peppers, even the aubergine. A lettuce should take seven weeks from start to finish, if you want something faster, try beansprouts – they take four days!

Nice 'N Easy

Beginners start here, please. Here are some plants that are so amiable, so easy to grow that it's almost impossible to kill them – that's our story, and we're sticking to it! We've excluded obvious items like cacti, which really can take care of themselves indefinitely, and gone for more conventional plants. If you've had no luck with growing plants indoors until now, try one of these:

Aglaonema (Chinese Evergreen)
This one is good in dim conditions, has two-tone light/dark green leaves.

Asparagus fern
Looks delicate, but is surprisingly tough. Pretty to use as a trailer, prefers some humidity, indirect sunlight. Not a true fern.

Aspidistra
The Victorians really knew what they were doing when they favoured this one. It's not called the Cast Iron Plant for nothing. It can cope with almost any conditions, especially cool and shady ones. It makes a good display piece too.

Chlorophytum (Spider Plant)
It's good natured, stands bright sun and shade with equal grace. Once it starts its production of plantlets on the end of those thin stems there's no stopping it.

Cissus antarctica (Kangaroo Vine)
It's a relation of the Virginia Creeper, a good basic climber to have around with its saw-edged shiny leaves.

Dracaena marginata
A fountain of dark green leaves makes this foliage plant a good accent piece. It appreciates good drainage. There is a very attractive variegated form – *D. marginata tricolor*.

Hedera (Ivy)
Good for cool rooms, underplanting among those showier items on the house-plant scene. *Hedera helix* is a trailer or climber.

Impatiens (Busy Lizzie)
Another good-tempered grower, gives you white or pink flowers, appreciates a little shade in high summer. Water it well.

Maranta (Prayer Plant)
A good mixer, with pleasant dark markings on its leaves which improve if kept away from too much light.

Pelargonium (Geranium)
Almost indestructible, this, but it can get very leggy if you don't pinch out the growing tips. Likes hot, sunny, dry conditions.

Philodendrons
Easy-going, amiable climbers to dress up a room. *Philodendron scandens*, with its glossy leaves, is the toughest type to choose.

Rhoicissus rhomboidea (Grape Ivy)
Another climber worth having, this one will stand dim light too.

Sansevieria (Mother-in-law's Tongue)
Rather a cheat, because it's actually a succulent. One of the easiest of all plants to grow, stands dry conditions and underwatering.

Tolmiea menziesii (Pick-a-back Plant)
Most prolific from the propagation point of view, it grows new plants abundantly where the leaves meet the stem.

Tradescantia (Wandering Sailor)
A cheap and cheerful give-away plant this, cuttings root easily in water. Keep it cropped to stop it getting leggy.

It's a Gift

Come Christmas-time, or birthdays, you can find yourself the recipient of a large, showy and apparently flourishing plant, gift-wrapped and yours – all yours. It's rather like finding a baby on your doorstep, and sometimes you don't even know its name. Caring for it under these conditions can become something of a problem. Gift plants are usually the more flamboyant ones, and most donors gravitate towards flowers, so the plant gift trade tends to run along certain well-trodden tracks. Most of us can expect to receive one of these, and here's how you look after them.

The big three are cyclamen, poinsettias and African violets, which have pages all their own in this book (34, 35 and 42, respectively). Don't panic, incidentally, if they look a little

unhappy to begin with. Being transported from a shop or nursery can make them look a little limp and sad at first – that's when we're tempted to overwater them. However, if they're kept out of sudden temperature changes or draughts, they will settle, even though it may take a week or so.

Anthuriums, sometimes called Wax, or Flamingo Flowers, are unmistakable because they look totally unreal. The plastic-like lipstick-red flowers, which are lily-like in shape, aren't really flowers at all; like the Poinsettia, they are modified leaves. Although they're really warm greenhouse plants in most climates, anthuriums will adapt to normal room temperatures. But they hate direct sunlight, so be warned. This is a plant that hates really hot, dry conditions.

Calceolarias make a popular present, you can't mistake their very exotic speckled, almost kidney-shaped flowers. These, again, are usually professionally grown to flower in the winter and then be thrown away. Keep them moist, or they will tend to drop their flowers.

Chrysanthemums, as pot plants, are now completely commercially controlled by lighting and chemicals to come dwarf size, and flower out of season. Enjoy them for the six weeks or so that they are in flower, then plant them out in the garden, and they will revert to type.

Cinerarias are another pop gift plant, flowering as they do from winter into spring. You should be able to keep the flowers going for up to six weeks, and they certainly make a colourful show with their bright flowers ranging from red to purple. Once they've finished, don't be disappointed if they just die down, they're disposable plants which are treated as annuals and should be thrown away.

Index